LAS VEGAS
TAVEL GUIDE
2025

Your Updated Insider's Guide to Sin City's
Best-Kept Secrets & Hottest Spots

CYRUS SEAFARER

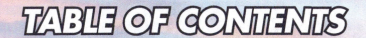

TABLE OF CONTENTS

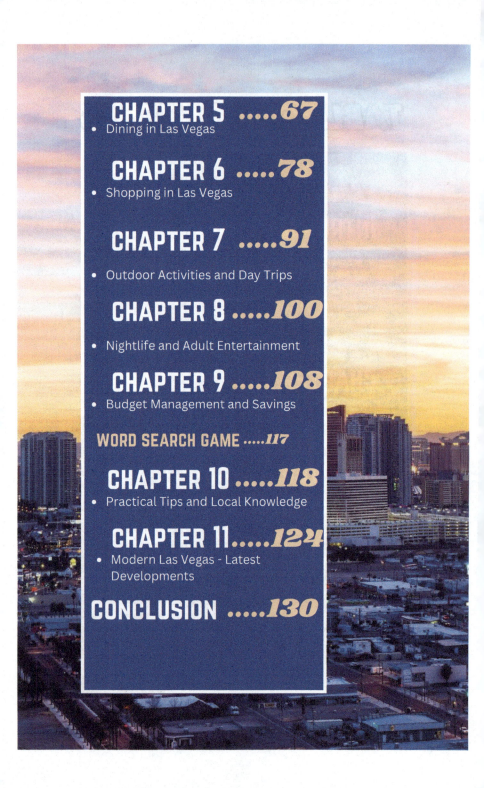

INTRODUCTION
Welcome to the Entertainment Capital of the World

Las Vegas beckons with a promise unlike any other city on Earth – a promise of unlimited possibilities, world-class entertainment, and memories that will last a lifetime. Whether you're drawn by the dazzling lights of the Strip, the culinary masterpieces of celebrity chefs, the thrill of world-class shows, or the natural wonders that surround this desert jewel, Las Vegas stands ready to exceed your expectations.

In this guide, we'll unlock the secrets of this remarkable destination, helping you navigate everything from the iconic casino resorts to hidden local gems. Las Vegas is no longer just a gambling destination; it has transformed into a multifaceted entertainment metropolis offering experiences for every type of traveler. From families seeking adventure to couples planning a romantic getaway, from food enthusiasts to outdoor adventurers, Las Vegas has carefully crafted experiences to delight every visitor

The Evolution of Las Vegas

From Desert Outpost to Global Entertainment Hub

What began as a dusty railroad stop in the Mojave Desert has blossomed into one of the world's most captivating destinations. Las Vegas's transformation is a testament to American ingenuity and ambition. In the early 1900s, the completion of the railroad between Los Angeles and Salt Lake City brought the first steady stream of visitors to this desert oasis. However, it was the legalization of gambling in Nevada in 1931 and the construction of the Hoover Dam that truly set the stage for Las Vegas's meteoric rise.

The 1940s and 50s saw the birth of the Strip, as visionaries like Bugsy Siegel and Howard Hughes recognized the potential for creating an entertainment paradise in the desert. What followed was decades of continuous reinvention, as Las Vegas evolved from a mob-connected gambling town to a corporate-run entertainment empire. Each era brought new innovations: the Rat Pack's sophisticated swagger in the 60s, the family-friendly turn of the 90s, and the luxury resort boom of the 2000s.

Today's Las Vegas stands as a testament to this constant evolution. The city has masterfully balanced its storied past with cutting-edge innovations, creating an experience that honors its history while embracing the future.

6

Why Las Vegas Continues to Captivate Millions

The Psychology of Endless Possibility

Las Vegas has mastered the art of perpetual reinvention while maintaining its core appeal: the promise of the extraordinary. Unlike other destinations that might offer a single draw—be it beaches, historical sites, or natural wonders—Las Vegas presents a kaleidoscope of experiences that change with each visit. This constant evolution ensures that even frequent visitors find something new to discover, creating an endless cycle of anticipation and fulfillment.

A City of Contrasts

The juxtaposition of experiences in Las Vegas creates an intoxicating blend of possibilities. Within a single day, visitors can lounge at a Mediterranean-style pool, dine at a Parisian café, watch an acclaimed Broadway show, and try their luck at games of chance. The city masterfully balances luxury with accessibility, offering both exclusive high-end experiences and affordable entertainment options that appeal to every budget.

The Entertainment Innovation Hub

Las Vegas consistently pushes the boundaries of entertainment, hosting groundbreaking shows that combine technology, artistry, and human excellence. From the pioneering performances of Cirque du Soleil to state-of-the-art virtual reality experiences, the city remains at the forefront of entertainment innovation, giving visitors access to shows and experiences they won't find anywhere else in the world.

7

Cultural and Culinary Crossroads

The city has evolved into a global culinary destination, where world-renowned chefs showcase their finest creations. This gastronomic excellence, combined with an ever-expanding array of cultural attractions, museums, and art installations, has transformed Las Vegas into a sophisticated cultural hub that appeals to discerning travelers from around the globe.

How to Use This Guide

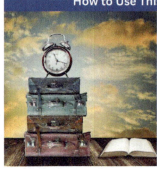

This guide is designed to grow with you as you plan your Las Vegas adventure. Each chapter builds upon the previous one, creating a comprehensive understanding of the city and its offerings. The content flows from essential orientation information to increasingly specialized knowledge, allowing you to dive as deeply as needed into any particular aspect of Las Vegas.

Making the Most of Interactive Elements

Throughout this guide, you'll find specially designed maps and interactive elements that enhance your learning experience. These tools are carefully placed to help you visualize locations, understand spatial relationships, and retain important information through engaging activities and puzzles.

Planning Your Reading Strategy

- **For First-Time Visitors**

Begin with Chapters 1-4 to build a strong foundation of knowledge about Las Vegas's layout, basic planning considerations, and essential experiences. These chapters provide the crucial information needed to start shaping your trip.

- **For Return Visitors**

If you've visited Las Vegas before, use the detailed table of contents to jump directly to sections covering new experiences or areas you haven't explored. The chapters on latest developments and modern Las Vegas will be particularly valuable for understanding recent changes.

What to Expect from Your Las Vegas Experience

Las Vegas captivates instantly with its glittering oasis amidst the desert. The four-mile-long Strip buzzes with slot machines, live music, and lively chatter. Open 24/7, the city lets you dine at midnight or catch a dawn show. Walking reveals a blend of casinos, shops, and attractions, while the contrast between dazzling fountains and Red Rock Canyon offers excitement and tranquility.

CHAPTER 1

Understanding Las Vegas's Geography and Layout

Before diving into the excitement and endless possibilities that Las Vegas offers, it's essential to understand the city's unique layout and geography. Las Vegas presents a fascinating study in urban planning, where entertainment, hospitality, and residential areas blend in a way unlike any other city in the world.

The desert metropolis has evolved from a single main street into a complex network of interconnected districts, each with its own distinct character and appeal. In this chapter, we'll explore the fundamental geography of Las Vegas, from the world-famous Strip to the historic downtown area, helping you develop a mental map that will serve as the foundation for all your Vegas adventures. Understanding this layout is crucial not just for navigation, but for maximizing your time and enjoying everything the city has to offer.

The Famous
LAS VEGAS
Strip

Las Vegas Boulevard South, universally known as "The Strip," serves as the grand stage where Las Vegas presents its most spectacular shows of architecture, entertainment, and human ingenuity. Stretching 4.2 miles from the Stratosphere Tower in the north to Mandalay Bay in the south, this iconic thoroughfare can be thought of as a series of interconnected neighborhoods, each with its own character and appeal.

Imagine the Strip as a necklace, with each resort representing a unique jewel connected by a thread of pedestrian walkways, bridges, and trams. To help you understand this layout, let's take a virtual walk from south to north, noting the distinctive features and landmarks that will help you navigate with confidence.

Our journey begins at the southern gateway, marked by the gleaming gold towers of Mandalay Bay. This tropical-themed resort marks the official beginning of the Strip experience, though you'll find other hotels and attractions further south. The resort's location provides an excellent reference point, particularly visible thanks to its distinctive gold-tinted windows that shimmer in the desert sun.

Moving north, you'll encounter what many consider the heart of the modern Strip—the stretch between Tropicana Avenue and Flamingo Road. This central section houses some of the most photographed scenes in Las Vegas. The dancing fountains of Bellagio perform their aquatic ballet directly across from the Egyptian pyramids of Luxor and the Manhattan skyline of New York-New York, creating a surreal world tour within a few city blocks.

Imagine the Strip as a necklace, with each resort representing a unique jewel connected by a thread of pedestrian walkways, bridges, and trams. To help you understand this layout, let's take a virtual walk from south to north, noting the distinctive features and landmarks that will help you navigate with confidence.

Our journey begins at the southern gateway, marked by the gleaming gold towers of Mandalay Bay. This tropical-themed resort marks the official beginning of the Strip experience, though you'll find other hotels and attractions further south. The resort's location provides an excellent reference point, particularly visible thanks to its distinctive gold-tinted windows that shimmer in the desert sun.

One of the most important things to understand about the Strip is its deceptive scale. What appears to be a short walk on a map can take considerably longer in reality. This is partly due to the desert heat, but mostly because of the Strip's unique pedestrian flow. The walkways intentionally meander through properties and around attractions, creating an immersive experience that encourages exploration but extends walking times.

Understanding the cross streets is crucial for navigation. Major intersections like Tropicana Avenue, Flamingo Road, and Sahara Avenue serve as primary reference points. These east-west arteries not only help with orientation but also provide access to off-Strip attractions and local neighborhoods. Each major intersection is marked by pedestrian bridges, making it easy to cross safely while offering excellent photo opportunities.

Climate considerations play a crucial role in Strip navigation. During summer months (May through September), the desert sun can be intense. Fortunately, the Strip's design incorporates numerous indoor passages and air-conditioned spaces.

Learning to utilize these climate-controlled routes can make your exploration much more comfortable.

Downtown Las Vegas and Fremont Street

When many visitors think they've seen all of Las Vegas after exploring the Strip, they're missing out on the city's historic heart and cultural soul: Downtown Las Vegas. Centered around Fremont Street, this district tells the story of where Las Vegas began and showcases where it's heading in the future. This is where the first hotel in Las Vegas opened its doors, where the first gaming license was issued, and where you can still find some of the most authentic Vegas experiences.

Fremont Street Experience, a five-block entertainment district, serves as downtown's crown jewel. The world's largest video screen spans the length of this pedestrian corridor, creating an immersive canopy of light and sound that illuminates the historic casino facades below. This 1,500-foot-long LED display delivers nightly light shows that transform the space into a stunning digital art gallery. Unlike the vastness of the Strip, downtown's more intimate scale creates an environment where everything feels accessible and interconnected.

The area surrounding Fremont Street has undergone a remarkable renaissance in recent years. The Arts District, affectionately known as "18b" by locals, has blossomed into a creative hub filled with galleries, vintage shops, and innovative dining spots.

Off-Strip
AREAS WORTH
Exploring

Las Vegas extends far beyond its famous tourist corridors, offering rewarding experiences for those willing to venture into its diverse neighborhoods and surrounding areas. Just a few miles west of the Strip, Chinatown Las Vegas presents an authentic Asian dining and shopping experience that spans multiple strip malls along Spring Mountain Road. This district has evolved into one of America's most exciting dining destinations, where you can find everything from high-end sushi to late-night dim sum.

Summerlin, nestled against the western edge of the valley, offers a different perspective on Las Vegas living. This master-planned community features outdoor shopping centers, championship golf courses, and easy access to Red Rock Canyon National Conservation Area. The area's Downtown Summerlin has become a destination in itself, with upscale shopping, dining, and entertainment options that rival those found on the Strip.

For those interested in history and nature, the Boulder City area, located about 30 minutes from the Strip, offers a fascinating glimpse into Nevada's past.

This town, built to house workers during the construction of Hoover Dam, maintains its historic charm and serves as a gateway to both the engineering marvel of the dam and the recreational paradise of Lake Mead. Boulder City's antique shops, museums, and small-town atmosphere provide a striking contrast to the glitz of the Strip.

If you're interested in outdoor recreation, the areas surrounding Las Vegas offer endless possibilities. Mount Charleston, less than an hour from downtown, provides an alpine escape where temperatures can be 20-30 degrees cooler than the valley. Here you'll find hiking trails, ski slopes (in winter), and scenic drives that make it hard to believe you're still in the Mojave Desert.

Transportation Infrastructure and Getting Around

Las Vegas has developed a sophisticated transportation network that connects its various districts and attractions, making it possible to explore the city in multiple ways. Understanding these transportation options will help you navigate the city efficiently and economically.

Airport Connections

Harry Reid International Airport (formerly McCarran) serves as the primary gateway to Las Vegas, situated conveniently just minutes from the Strip. Transportation options from the airport are plentiful, with each serving different needs and budgets. The taxi line might seem daunting, but it moves quickly and offers fixed rates to different hotel zones. Ride-sharing services operate from a dedicated pickup area at Terminal 1's Level 2M, providing an often more economical option. For those heading downtown, the airport shuttle services offer cost-effective transportation with multiple stop options.

Navigating The Strip

The Las Vegas Strip's transportation system is a marvel of convenience, combining various options to help visitors move efficiently between attractions. The Las Vegas Monorail runs along the east side of the Strip, connecting MGM Grand to Sahara Las Vegas with stops at major resorts along the way. This elevated train provides quick transportation while offering spectacular views of the city.

- **Free Tram Services**

Several free tram services connect specific resort groups:
1. The Mandalay Bay Tram connects Mandalay Bay, Luxor, and Excalibur
2. The ARIA Express serves Bellagio, Vdara, ARIA, and Park MGM
3. The Mirage-Treasure Island Tram connects these two neighboring resorts

- **Walking the Strip**

While walking remains popular, it's important to understand the pedestrian infrastructure. Elevated walkways and covered passages provide climate-controlled alternatives to street-level sidewalks. These walkways not only offer protection from the weather but also provide excellent vantage points for photography.

Weather Patterns and Best Times to Visit

Las Vegas's desert climate creates distinct seasonal patterns that can significantly impact your visit. Understanding these patterns helps you plan activities and pack appropriately for maximum comfort.

Desert Climate Dynamics

Located in the Mojave Desert, Las Vegas experiences dramatic temperature swings both seasonally and daily. Summer days can soar above 100°F (38°C), while winter nights can drop below freezing. This desert environment creates a unique climate pattern where temperatures can vary by 30 degrees or more between day and night.

- **Summer Season (June - September)**

Summer brings intense heat with daytime temperatures regularly exceeding 100°F (38°C). However, the dry climate means less discomfort than you might expect in humid regions. Early morning and evening hours become prime times for outdoor activities. Hotels and casinos maintain careful climate control, creating comfortable indoor environments regardless of outside temperatures.

Summer Survival Tips:

1. Plan outdoor activities for early morning or evening
2. Stay hydrated (many hotels provide complimentary water)
3. - Use indoor connections between properties during peak heat
4. Take advantage of pool areas, which are designed for desert comfort

- **Mild Seasons (March - May, October - November)**

Spring and fall offer the most comfortable weather for exploring Las Vegas. Daytime temperatures typically range from 70-85°F (21-29°C), perfect for outdoor activities and walking the Strip. These seasons also tend to have the clearest skies, ideal for photography and outdoor shows.

- **Winter Season (December - February)**

Winter brings mild daytime temperatures and cool nights. While snowfall is rare in the valley, the surrounding mountains often receive snow, creating spectacular views. This season sees some of the city's largest conventions and New Year celebrations, making advance planning essential.

Event-Based Timing Considerations

Beyond weather, several other factors influence the best time to visit:

1. Major conventions can impact hotel rates and availability
2. Pool season typically runs March through October
3. Holiday periods bring special events but also larger crowds

Major Districts
AND THEIR
Characteristics

Las Vegas is a tapestry of distinct districts, each with its own personality and appeal. Understanding these different areas helps you not only navigate the city but also discover experiences that match your interests. Think of Las Vegas as a collection of interconnected neighborhoods, each telling its own story while contributing to the larger narrative of this remarkable city.

The Resort Corridor

The famous Las Vegas Strip can be divided into three distinct sections, each with its own character. The South Strip, anchored by Mandalay Bay, embraces a modern luxury aesthetic with expansive resorts and upscale amenities. Here you'll find properties like Luxor and MGM Grand, where contemporary entertainment meets traditional casino gaming. The architecture in this section tends toward the sleek and sophisticated, with less emphasis on the themed designs of earlier eras.

Moving into the Central Strip, from Paris Las Vegas to Wynn, you'll encounter the heart of Las Vegas's most iconic experiences. This section hosts the city's most photographed attractions, including the Bellagio Fountains and the Eiffel Tower replica.

Historic Downtown District

Downtown Las Vegas deserves special attention as the city's original gambling district. Centered on Fremont Street, this area offers a more intimate Las Vegas experience. The historic casinos here, like the Golden Nugget and El Cortez, maintain lower table minimums and more favorable odds than their Strip counterparts. The district has evolved beyond gaming to become a cultural hub, with three distinct zones worth exploring.

The Fremont Street Experience serves as the entertainment core, where the world's largest video canopy creates an immersive light show each night. Adjacent to this, Fremont East has emerged as the city's hipster haven, with craft cocktail bars, vintage shops, and innovative restaurants occupying restored mid-century buildings. The nearby Arts District, spanning 18 blocks, has become a creative incubator for local artists, featuring galleries, antique shops, and some of the city's most exciting new restaurants.

Local Living Districts

Beyond the tourist corridors, Las Vegas's residential districts offer insight into local life and often-overlooked attractions. Summerlin, in the western valley, represents upscale suburban living with its master-planned communities, championship golf courses, and outdoor shopping districts. The area's proximity to Red Rock Canyon makes it a favorite among outdoor enthusiasts.

Henderson, to the southeast, has developed its own distinct identity with family-friendly attractions and outdoor recreation areas. The Green Valley area within Henderson features upscale shopping centers and some of the valley's best restaurants away from the Strip. The Water Street District, Henderson's historic core, has undergone remarkable revitalization to become a destination for craft beer enthusiasts and food lovers.

Cultural Corridors

Las Vegas's Chinatown, stretching along Spring Mountain Road, has grown far beyond its name to become one of America's most diverse Pan-Asian districts. What began as a single shopping plaza has expanded into a miles-long corridor of authentic Asian restaurants, markets, and cultural centers.

The Maryland Parkway corridor, connecting the University of Nevada Las Vegas to downtown, represents the city's educational and cultural spine. This district hosts an eclectic mix of vintage shops, international restaurants, and independent businesses catering to the student population. The area's recent revitalization has brought new energy to historic neighborhoods like Paradise Palms, showcasing Las Vegas's mid-century modern architectural heritage.

Entertainment Districts Beyond the Strip

The city has developed several entertainment districts that operate independently of the major resorts. Town Square, south of the Strip, creates an outdoor shopping and dining experience that appeals to both tourists and locals. Similarly, Downtown Summerlin has emerged as a destination in itself, offering high-end retail and dining options in an open-air setting that takes advantage of Las Vegas's climate.

Understanding these distinct districts helps you appreciate Las Vegas's complexity and find experiences that might otherwise be overlooked. Each area offers its own perspective on the city, from the high-energy tourist corridors to peaceful suburban communities, from historic neighborhoods to ultra-modern developments.

CHAPTER 2

Planning Your Trip - Essential
Preparations

Planning a trip to Las Vegas requires thoughtful consideration of various factors that will shape your experience in this multifaceted city. While spontaneity certainly has its place in Las Vegas, a well-planned trip ensures you'll make the most of your time and budget while experiencing everything that interests you most. In this chapter, we'll explore the essential elements of trip planning, from determining the ideal length of your stay to managing your budget effectively. Whether you're planning your first visit or returning for a new adventure, these preparations will help you create a memorable Las Vegas experience that aligns with your expectations and desires.

Optimal Duration for Different Types of Visits

The ideal length of your Las Vegas stay depends largely on your interests, goals, and travel style. Understanding how different durations suit various types of visits will help you plan a trip that feels neither rushed nor overextended.

For first-time visitors, a minimum of three nights allows you to experience the essential elements of Las Vegas. This duration gives you time to explore the Strip's major attractions, enjoy a few shows, and sample the city's renowned dining scene while maintaining a comfortable pace. You'll have enough time to adjust to the unique rhythm of Las Vegas and experience both daytime and nighttime attractions.

Business travelers combining work with leisure might find a four to five-night stay ideal. This duration accommodates professional commitments while leaving time for entertainment and relaxation. The extra days allow you to transition smoothly between business and leisure activities, perhaps enjoying pool time in the morning before meetings or shows in the evening after conference sessions.

For those seeking a deeper Las Vegas experience, a week-long stay opens up possibilities beyond the Strip. This duration allows you to explore downtown Las Vegas, venture into local neighborhoods, and take day trips to nearby attractions like Red Rock Canyon or Hoover Dam. A longer stay also gives you the flexibility to pace yourself, preventing the exhaustion that can come from trying to pack too much into a short visit.

Special events and celebrations might require adjusting these timeframes. Wedding parties often find that a three to four-night stay works well, allowing time for the ceremony, celebration, and recovery. Convention attendees should consider adding two to three leisure days beyond their business commitments to experience the city properly.

Weekend visitors can still have a fulfilling experience, but should focus their itinerary on specific priorities. A carefully planned 48-hour visit can include a show, fine dining experiences, and exploration of the Strip's attractions. However, weekend visitors should be prepared for larger crowds and higher room rates, as Friday and Saturday nights are typically the busiest and most expensive.

Season and weather also influence the optimal duration of your stay. Summer visitors might prefer shorter stays of three to four nights due to the intense heat, planning indoor activities during peak temperatures. Spring and fall visitors often opt for longer stays to take advantage of comfortable temperatures ideal for outdoor exploration.

For those interested in the culinary scene, consider that Las Vegas's top restaurants often book up weeks in advance. A stay of five nights or more gives you the flexibility to secure reservations at multiple sought-after venues while still having time for spontaneous dining discoveries.

Adventure seekers planning to explore beyond the city should consider stays of a week or longer. This allows time to combine the excitement of Las Vegas with outdoor activities in the surrounding desert landscape, creating a varied and dynamic vacation experience.

Remember that Las Vegas can be both energizing and exhausting. The constant stimulation, walking distances, and potential time zone adjustments affect everyone differently. Building in rest days during longer stays helps maintain your energy and enjoyment throughout the visit. These quieter days can be spent enjoying your hotel's pool, visiting a spa, or simply observing the fascinating parade of humanity that makes Las Vegas unique.

Budgeting Fundamentals:

Understanding Vegas Pricing

Las Vegas has a fascinating pricing structure that can seem contradictory at first glance. You might find a luxury hotel room for under $100 one night and over $500 the next, or encounter a world-class restaurant offering both $25 lunch specials and $500 tasting menus. Understanding these pricing dynamics will help you budget effectively and find value at every price point.

Hotel Pricing Dynamics

The foundation of Las Vegas budgeting starts with understanding hotel pricing. Room rates fluctuate dramatically based on several factors working in combination. Weekends typically command higher rates than weekdays, with Friday and Saturday nights often priced at double or triple the Sunday through Thursday rates. Major conventions, fight nights, and special events can cause prices to spike across all properties. Conversely, summer weekdays and post-New Year periods often offer exceptional values.

Resort fees deserve special attention in your budgeting. These mandatory daily charges range from $30 to $50 or more per room and are not included in the advertised room rate.

Entertainment and Shows

Show tickets represent another significant expense where strategic planning matters. Booking directly through hotel box offices can mean paying full retail prices, often $100-200 per person for major productions. However, same-day discount ticket booths (known as "Tix4Tonight") can offer savings of 30-50% if you're flexible about show times and seating. For must-see shows, especially limited engagements or celebrity performances, advance booking at full price might be your only option.

Dining Costs

Las Vegas dining costs span an enormous range. Budget-conscious travelers can find excellent meals at under $20 per person, while luxury dining experiences can easily exceed $200 per person. Many high-end restaurants offer more affordable lunch menus, presenting an opportunity to experience premium venues at a fraction of dinner prices. Hotel breakfast buffets typically range from $25-40 per person, while dinner buffets can range from $40-70.

Transportation Considerations

Transportation costs often surprise first-time visitors. While walking is free, Las Vegas distances can make ride-sharing or taxis necessary. A ride from the airport to Strip hotels typically costs $25-35, while trips between Strip locations usually range from $10-20.

Making Advance
RESERVATIONS:
What and When

Knowing when to make different types of reservations can be as important as understanding what they'll cost. Las Vegas operates on various booking windows that require different planning horizons for optimal results.

Hotel Reservations Timing

Hotel reservations should typically be made 2-3 months in advance for the best combination of availability and pricing. This window allows you to monitor rates and take advantage of promotional offers while ensuring you secure your preferred property. For major events or holidays like New Year's Eve, extend this to 4-6 months. Most hotels offer free cancellation until 48-72 hours before arrival, allowing you to book early and continue watching for better rates.

Restaurant Booking Strategies

Premium restaurants in Las Vegas often book up weeks or even months in advance, particularly for prime dinner times between 6:30 and 8:30 PM. Many high-end establishments open reservations 60-90 days ahead, and popular venues like Hell's Kitchen or é by José Andrés can fill up within hours of releasing tables. For such destinations, set calendar reminders for when booking windows open.

Fine dining reservations generally fall into three tiers:

- 90 days: Ultra-premium venues and chef's table experiences
- 60 days: Most fine dining restaurants and popular celebrity chef venues
- 30 days: Casual upscale restaurants and busy Strip locations

Show Ticket Timing

Show tickets require different strategies depending on the type of performance. For resident shows like Cirque du Soleil productions, booking 1-2 months ahead usually suffices and might reveal early booking discounts. Limited engagement performances, especially by popular artists, might require purchasing as soon as tickets go on sale, sometimes 6 months or more in advance.

Special Experience Reservations

Unique experiences like spa treatments, golf tee times, or specialty dining (like exclusive chef's tables) often have their own booking windows:

- Spa treatments: 2-4 weeks ahead, longer for holidays
- Golf tee times: Up to 90 days for premium courses
- Special dining experiences: 60-90 days, sometimes more for holidays

Transportation Options To and From Las Vegas

Understanding your transportation options to and from Las Vegas is crucial for a smooth travel experience. Harry Reid International Airport serves as the primary gateway to the city, handling millions of visitors annually with remarkable efficiency. Let's explore the various ways to reach Las Vegas and how to navigate your arrival and departure effectively.

Air Travel Considerations

Flying into Las Vegas offers convenience and often the best value for travelers coming from distances greater than 300 miles. The airport's location, just minutes from the Strip, makes it one of the most conveniently situated major airports in the United States. When booking flights, consider that midweek arrivals and departures typically offer better rates than weekend travel. Many airlines increase their flight frequency to Las Vegas during major conventions and events, though prices tend to rise during these periods.

Ground Transportation Services

Driving to Las Vegas remains popular for visitors from nearby states, particularly California, Arizona, and Utah. The city's major highways are well-maintained and clearly marked, though desert conditions require some extra preparation. If you're driving from Southern California, be aware that weekend traffic on Interstate 15 can add several hours to your journey, especially on Friday afternoons heading to Vegas and Sunday afternoons returning to California.

Bus services provide an economical option for budget-conscious travelers. Companies like Greyhound operate regular routes to Las Vegas from major Western cities, with some buses offering WiFi and power outlets. For Southern California residents, several shuttle services operate daily trips specifically designed for Vegas visitors, often including hotel drop-off and pickup services.

Airport to Hotel Transportation

Once you arrive at Harry Reid International Airport, several transportation options await. The airport's design places a premium on efficient movement of arriving passengers to their final destinations:

The taxi line, while sometimes appearing long, moves quickly due to well-organized dispatching. Taxis use a zone-based fare system for Strip and downtown hotels, helping prevent overcharging through longer routes. For groups of three or four people, taxis often prove as economical as shared shuttle services.

Ride-sharing services like Uber and Lyft operate from designated pickup areas at both terminals. These services typically offer lower fares than taxis but may implement surge pricing during peak periods. The dedicated pickup areas include clear signage and queue systems to help you find your driver efficiently.

Shuttle services provide economical shared transportation, particularly beneficial for solo travelers or couples. While shuttles take longer than taxis or ride-shares due to multiple stops, they offer significant savings.

Travel Insurance and Health Considerations

Protecting your health and travel investment requires careful consideration of both insurance coverage and environmental factors unique to Las Vegas. The city's desert location and round-the-clock activity create specific challenges that visitors should prepare for.

Travel Insurance Essentials

Travel insurance for Las Vegas trips deserves special consideration due to several factors. The city's popularity for celebrations and special events means many travelers book expensive show tickets or special experience packages in advance. Look for policies that cover not just trip cancellation but also entertainment ticket protection. Many premium credit cards offer some travel insurance benefits, but review the coverage carefully, especially for show tickets and special events.

Consider that Las Vegas trips often involve higher discretionary spending than typical vacations. Some travel insurance policies offer coverage for casino chips or gaming losses due to theft or robbery, though carefully review the terms and documentation requirements for such claims.

Health Preparations and Considerations

The desert environment of Las Vegas requires specific health preparations. The arid climate can cause rapid dehydration, often before visitors notice symptoms. Plan to drink significantly more water than you might at home, even if you're not feeling particularly thirsty.

The contrast between hot outdoor temperatures and heavily air-conditioned indoor spaces can stress your system, so consider carrying a light jacket even in summer.

Medical Services and Accessibility

Las Vegas offers excellent medical facilities, with several major hospitals and numerous urgent care centers. Most major hotels have relationships with nearby medical providers and can quickly arrange care if needed. If you require regular medical treatments, such as dialysis, research facilities near your hotel and make arrangements in advance.

For visitors with mobility challenges, Las Vegas has made significant strides in accessibility. Most major properties offer excellent wheelchair access, and many show venues have dedicated spaces for guests with mobility devices. However, the sheer size of casino resorts means significant distances between venues, so plan accordingly and inquire about mobility scooter rentals if needed.

Essential Apps and Digital Tools

for Vegas Visitors

The digital age has transformed how we experience Las Vegas, with technology making it easier than ever to navigate, plan, and enhance your visit. Understanding and utilizing these digital tools can significantly improve your Vegas experience, helping you save time, money, and avoid common frustrations. Let's explore the essential digital resources that will help you make the most of your time in the Entertainment Capital of the World.

Resort and Casino Applications

Major resort groups in Las Vegas have developed comprehensive mobile applications that serve as digital concierges for their properties. These apps typically allow you to manage reservations, check in to your room, make dining bookings, and even unlock your hotel room door with your smartphone. Before your visit, download the appropriate apps for the resorts where you'll be staying or visiting. Many of these applications also offer exclusive deals and promotions not available through other channels.

What to look for in resort apps:
- Digital room key capabilities
- Restaurant reservation systems
- Show ticket purchasing options
- Resort maps and directions
- Loyalty program integration

37

Navigation Tools

Las Vegas's unique layout and massive resort complexes can be challenging to navigate. Modern mapping applications have developed specialized features for Las Vegas, including indoor mapping of major resorts and walking directions that account for pedestrian bridges and trams. When using navigation apps in Las Vegas, enable the walking directions feature, as it often provides more accurate travel time estimates and better routing through casino properties.

Consider downloading offline maps before your arrival, as indoor casino coverage can be spotty. Look for navigation tools that include:

- Indoor resort mapping
- Pedestrian bridge routes
- Public transportation integration
- Points of interest along walking routes
- Estimated walking times between destinations

Ride-Sharing and Transportation

Transportation apps have become essential tools for Las Vegas visitors. These services can help you avoid long taxi lines and often provide more predictable pricing. Many transportation apps now include features specifically designed for Las Vegas, such as designated pickup locations at hotels and venues.

Dining and Entertainment Resources

Several digital platforms specialize in helping visitors discover and book dining and entertainment options in Las Vegas. These tools often provide detailed reviews, photos, and the ability to make reservations directly through the application. Look for platforms that offer:

- Real-time restaurant availability
- Show schedules and ticket purchasing
- User reviews and photos
- Special event calendars
- Happy hour listings
- Last-minute dining deals

Weather and Environmental Tools

The desert environment of Las Vegas makes weather apps particularly important. Look for applications that provide:

- UV index forecasts
- Air quality information
- Heat advisories
- Pool condition updates
- Indoor/outdoor temperature differentials
- Severe weather alerts

Planning and Organization Tools

Digital planning tools can help coordinate complex Vegas itineraries. Consider applications that offer:

- Customizable schedules
- Reservation management
- Ticket organization
- Group coordination features
- Budget tracking
- Packing lists

Digital Security Considerations

When using digital tools in Las Vegas, maintain good security practices:

- Use secure, password-protected WiFi networks
- Enable two-factor authentication
- Keep software updated
- Back up important documents
- Monitor account activity
- Use secure payment methods

Remember that while digital tools can enhance your Vegas experience, they should complement rather than replace common sense and personal interaction. Many visitors find that a combination of digital resources and traditional planning methods works best for making the most of their Las Vegas adventure.

CHAPTER 3
Accommodation Strategies

Choosing where to stay in Las Vegas is perhaps the most crucial decision you'll make when planning your visit. Your accommodation choice influences not only your comfort but also shapes your entire Vegas experience. The right hotel puts you close to your preferred activities, matches your budget and style preferences, and provides the amenities that matter most to you. In this chapter, we'll explore the intricacies of Las Vegas accommodations, from luxury resorts to boutique hotels, helping you make an informed decision that enhances your stay in this remarkable city.

Understanding Hotel Categories and Districts

Las Vegas hotels are as diverse as the city itself, each offering a unique blend of amenities, atmosphere, and experiences. To make an informed choice, it's helpful to understand how these properties are categorized and what each district offers. Think of Las Vegas hotels as existing within distinct tiers and locations, each serving different travel styles and preferences.

Luxury Category Properties

The luxury tier in Las Vegas redefines opulence, offering experiences that rival or exceed the finest hotels worldwide. These properties, such as those in the Wynn and Bellagio families, are characterized by impeccable service, sophisticated design, and premium amenities. In these establishments, you'll find spacious rooms with high-end furnishings, marble bathrooms, and views that showcase the city's splendor. The dining options typically include restaurants from world-renowned chefs, while the spa facilities offer comprehensive wellness experiences.

What sets luxury properties apart in Las Vegas is their attention to detail. You'll notice it in the fresh flowers that adorn public spaces, the custom fragrances that perfume the air, and the staff who seem to anticipate your needs before you express them. These hotels generally command the highest rates but often deliver value through included amenities and services that would cost extra elsewhere.

Premium Mid-Tier Properties

The premium mid-tier represents excellent quality without the ultra-luxury price tag. These properties offer upscale experiences with a focus on specific themes or atmospheres. You'll find well-appointed rooms, multiple dining options, and engaging entertainment venues. The service level remains high, though perhaps not as personalized as in luxury properties. These hotels often provide the best balance of quality and value for many visitors.

Think of premium mid-tier properties as offering most of the amenities you'd want in a Vegas vacation—comfortable rooms, good restaurants, attractive pools, and central locations—without some of the more elaborate features of luxury properties. They're ideal for travelers who want a high-quality experience but plan to spend significant time exploring beyond their hotel.

Value-Oriented Properties

Value properties in Las Vegas often surprise visitors with their quality level. Unlike value hotels in many other cities, Las Vegas's competitive market means that even lower-priced properties must maintain appealing standards to attract guests. These hotels typically offer clean, comfortable rooms and basic amenities, with their main advantage being price and often location.

Many value properties have undergone recent renovations to remain competitive, resulting in rooms that might exceed expectations for their price point.

Location Categories

The location of your hotel plays a crucial role in your Las Vegas experience. The city's hotel districts each offer distinct advantages:

Center Strip locations put you in the heart of the action, with easy walking access to major attractions. These hotels often command premium prices but save time and transportation costs. They're ideal for first-time visitors who want to experience the essence of Las Vegas.

North and South Strip properties often offer better value while still providing Strip access. They require more walking or transportation to reach central attractions but can provide quieter environments and often larger rooms for the price. These locations work well for return visitors who know their preferred activities and don't mind some additional travel time.

Off-Strip hotels, including those near the Convention Center or in downtown Las Vegas, present unique advantages. Downtown properties put you close to Fremont Street's historic casinos and cultural attractions, often at lower prices than Strip hotels. Convention Center area hotels cater well to business travelers while offering easy monorail access to the Strip.

Strip Hotels:
COMPREHENSIVE
Analysis and Comparisons

The Las Vegas Strip presents a fascinating array of accommodation options, each with its own personality and appeal. To truly understand these properties, we need to look beyond their glittering facades and examine what makes each unique. Let's explore how different Strip hotels serve different types of travelers and what makes each property special.

The South Strip cluster, anchored by Mandalay Bay, offers a more relaxed atmosphere compared to the central Strip. Mandalay Bay's tropical theme extends beyond mere decoration to create a genuine resort experience, complete with a sand-and-surf beach complex and wave pool. The connected properties of Luxor and Excalibur create a value corridor, with each step north generally offering lower rates while maintaining decent amenities. These hotels work particularly well for families and travelers who prefer a slightly quieter environment while maintaining easy access to the heart of the Strip.

The central Strip presents the highest concentration of luxury properties, with each trying to outdo the others in terms of amenities and experiences. Bellagio sets the standard for luxury with its Mediterranean elegance, famous fountains, and high-end gaming areas.

Downtown and Off-Strip Options

Downtown Las Vegas offers a compelling alternative to Strip accommodations, with properties that combine historical charm with modern amenities. The Golden Nugget stands out as downtown's flagship property, offering amenities that rival Strip hotels, including a unique pool complex featuring a shark tank and waterslide. The property maintains high standards while generally offering better value than comparable Strip hotels.

The Downtown Grand and Circa represent downtown's evolution, bringing modern amenities and design to the Fremont Street area. Circa, in particular, has redefined expectations for downtown properties with its sophisticated rooms and expansive pool complex. These newer properties prove that staying downtown no longer means sacrificing quality or amenities.

Off-Strip properties fall into several distinct categories. The Rio and Palms offer full-resort experiences with the advantage of Strip views from most rooms, thanks to their slightly removed locations. These properties often provide larger rooms and better values, though transportation considerations become more important.

Resort Fees and Hidden Costs Explained

Understanding the true cost of a Las Vegas hotel stay requires looking beyond the advertised room rate. Resort fees represent the most significant hidden cost, having become standard practice across most Las Vegas properties. These mandatory daily charges range from $25 to $50 or more per room and significantly impact your total cost.

What makes resort fees particularly challenging is that they often cover amenities you might expect to be included in the room rate, such as:
- Internet access
- Local phone calls
- Fitness center access
- Pool access
- In-room coffee makers
- Printing of boarding passe

Beyond resort fees, several other potential costs require consideration. Parking fees have become common at Strip properties, with rates varying between self-parking and valet services. While some hotels still offer free parking to local residents or high-tier loyalty members, most visitors should factor in daily parking costs of $15-30.

Room type and view premiums can significantly affect your rate. Strip-view rooms typically command $30-50 more per night than mountain-view or parking-lot-view rooms.

High-floor premiums, special room types (like spa suites or fountain-view rooms), and weekend rates can all add substantially to your base rate.

Mini-bar and in-room amenity charges require special attention. Many Las Vegas hotel rooms now feature "smart" mini-bars that automatically charge your account if items are moved, even if not consumed. Some rooms also have sensors that charge for snacks placed on certain surfaces, so be careful about where you put personal items.

However, savvy travelers can often mitigate these costs through various strategies:
Loyalty program membership often provides resort fee waivers or reductions
Booking packages that include resort fees can offer better overall value
Some third-party booking sites occasionally offer resort-fee-free promotions
Longer stays might qualify for reduced daily resort fees
Many properties offer dining credits or other amenities that can offset fees

When comparing hotel options, create a true daily cost calculation that includes:
- Base room rate
- Resort fee
- Estimated parking costs
- Any view or room type premiums
- Taxes (currently approximately 13.38% in Las Vegas)

Loyalty Programs
AND MAXIMIZING
Benefits

Understanding Las Vegas loyalty programs can transform your experience from ordinary to extraordinary. These programs have evolved far beyond simple gambling rewards, now encompassing every aspect of your stay. The major casino groups have developed sophisticated rewards systems that recognize both gaming and non-gaming spending, making them valuable even for visitors who rarely or never gamble.

These programs typically operate on a tier system, where your status level determines your benefits. The basic tier, available free to anyone who signs up, often provides immediate benefits like discounted room rates and special promotional offers. As you progress to higher tiers through spending or gameplay, the benefits expand significantly. These can include room upgrades, priority check-in lines, exclusive restaurant reservations, and even dedicated casino hosts who can arrange special experiences.

Smart visitors often join multiple loyalty programs before their trip, even if they plan to stay at just one property. This strategy opens up more dining and entertainment options, as many venues offer discounts to members regardless of their tier level.

Special Considerations for Extended Stays

Extended stays in Las Vegas require a different approach to both selection and strategy. When planning a longer visit, factors that might be minor inconveniences for a weekend become significant considerations. The location of your room relative to amenities like quiet corridors, ice machines, and elevator banks takes on greater importance. The availability of in-room amenities such as refrigerators, coffee makers, and adequate storage space becomes crucial for comfort.

For stays longer than a week, consider suite-style accommodations that offer separate living areas and basic kitchen facilities. Many properties offer these options, though they're not always well-advertised. Extended-stay guests should also investigate properties that cater to long-term visitors, often found slightly off-Strip. These typically offer larger rooms, better work spaces, and amenities more suited to longer stays.

Transportation becomes a more significant factor during extended stays. While Strip location might seem ideal, properties near efficient public transportation or with good parking facilities often prove more practical for longer visits.

Latest Trends in Vegas Accommodations

Las Vegas hotels continue to evolve, responding to changing traveler preferences and technological advances. The modern Las Vegas room increasingly emphasizes technology integration, with mobile check-in becoming standard and smartphone room keys growing in popularity. Many properties now offer apps that control room features like lighting, temperature, and entertainment systems, creating a more personalized experience.

Wellness has emerged as a major focus, with properties developing more sophisticated fitness centers and spa facilities. Some hotels now offer in-room fitness equipment or wellness programs, while others have created specialized "wellness rooms" featuring air purification systems, dawn simulation lighting, and ergonomic furniture.

Sustainability initiatives have become increasingly prominent. Many properties now employ advanced energy management systems, water conservation programs, and waste reduction strategies. These efforts extend beyond basic environmental considerations to include locally sourced restaurant ingredients and eco-friendly room products.

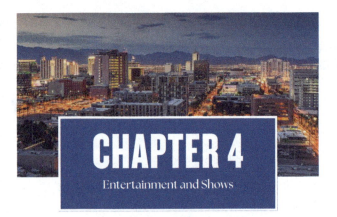

CHAPTER 4
Entertainment and Shows

Las Vegas has earned its reputation as the Entertainment Capital of the World through decades of pushing creative boundaries and consistently delivering world-class performances. The city's entertainment landscape offers an unprecedented variety of shows that cater to every taste and interest imaginable. From spectacular production shows that defy gravity to intimate musical performances that touch the soul, Las Vegas stages host some of the most innovative and captivating entertainment found anywhere in the world. In this chapter, we'll explore the diverse array of shows available and help you understand how to choose and book the performances that will make your visit truly memorable.

Understanding the Show Categories

Las Vegas shows can be categorized in several ways, each offering distinct experiences that appeal to different audiences. Understanding these categories helps you make informed choices about which shows will best match your interests and expectations.

Production shows represent the pinnacle of Las Vegas entertainment, combining multiple performance elements into cohesive theatrical experiences. These shows often feature elaborate sets, custom-built theaters, and large casts performing complex choreography. The production value of these shows rivals or exceeds what you might find on Broadway, with the added advantage of theaters designed specifically for each performance. These shows typically run nightly with occasional dark days for maintenance and performer rest.

Cirque du Soleil productions deserve special mention as they've created their own subcategory of entertainment. These shows blend acrobatics, dance, and theatrical elements with cutting-edge technology and artistic vision. Each Cirque show has its own theme and personality, from the aquatic wonderland of "O" to the rock-and-roll energy of "Love." What sets these productions apart is their ability to create immersive environments where every element, from the music to the staging, contributes to the overall experience.

Magic shows in Las Vegas range from grand illusions in custom theaters to intimate close-up performances in smaller venues. The city has long been a magnet for the world's top magicians, who often develop special effects and illusions specifically for their Las Vegas shows. These performances can vary from family-friendly entertainment to more sophisticated evening shows that blend magic with comedy or drama.

Comedy shows offer everything from stand-up performances by national touring acts to resident comedians who develop Vegas-specific material. Many hotels feature dedicated comedy clubs that offer nightly shows, while larger venues host well-known comedians for limited engagements. The comedy scene in Las Vegas is unique because performers often tailor their material to the city's diverse international audience.

Musical performances in Las Vegas span an incredible range, from solo pianists in intimate lounges to full orchestral productions in grand theaters. The city has become a preferred venue for musicians looking to create specialized shows that they couldn't perform while touring, allowing for more elaborate productions with fixed staging and effects.

MGM GRAND GARDEN ARENA

MGM Grand Garden Arena

3799 S Las Vegas Blvd, Las Vegas, NV 89109

4.5 ★★★★★ 3,873 reviews

View larger map

Directions

SCAN QR CODE

- Open your phone's camera app and point to the QR code
- Wait for your camera to recognize the QR code
- Tap the notification or banner that appears to open the encoded link

55

Resident Performances
AND LIMITED
Engagements

The concept of resident performances has evolved significantly in Las Vegas, creating a new standard for extended artistic engagements. Resident shows allow performers to develop more sophisticated productions than would be possible on tour, as they can utilize permanent technical installations and complex staging elements. These shows often represent the most polished version of an artist's vision, crafted specifically for their Vegas venue.

Modern residencies typically feature major recording artists performing runs of shows spread throughout the year. This format allows performers to maintain touring schedules while establishing a home base in Las Vegas. For visitors, resident shows offer the chance to see favorite artists in unique presentations designed specifically for Vegas audiences. These shows often include elements that wouldn't be possible in a touring production, from elaborate stage effects to rare songs and special guest appearances.

Limited engagements, on the other hand, bring fresh energy to the entertainment landscape. These shorter runs might feature Broadway shows, touring productions, or special performances by artists testing the waters for potential residencies.

Cirque du Soleil Productions

Cirque du Soleil has revolutionized Las Vegas entertainment, creating a new standard for theatrical productions that blend artistry, athleticism, and technological innovation. Since their first permanent Las Vegas show in 1993, Cirque du Soleil has consistently pushed the boundaries of what's possible in live entertainment, developing custom theaters that enable performances that couldn't exist anywhere else in the world.

Each Cirque du Soleil production in Las Vegas tells its own unique story through a distinctive combination of acrobatics, music, and theatrical elements. The shows are designed to be understood and appreciated regardless of language, making them accessible to Las Vegas's international audience. The productions typically run between 90 minutes and two hours, creating complete evening entertainment experiences that leave audiences amazed at human potential.

The aquatic production "O" at Bellagio demonstrates the unprecedented scale of these shows. The custom-built theater houses a 1.5-million-gallon pool that transforms from deep water to solid stage in seconds, allowing performers to seamlessly transition between underwater and above-ground sequences.

"O" by Cirque du Soleil

3600 S L[...]
NV 8910[...]
4.6 ★★★

View larger map

CIRQUE DU SOLEIL

SCAN QR CODE

- Open your phone's camera app and point to the QR code
- Wait for your camera to recognize the QR code
- Tap the notification or banner that appears to open the encoded link

Magic Shows and Comedy Acts

Las Vegas has long been synonymous with world-class magic, attracting the finest practitioners of this art form to create groundbreaking shows. Modern Las Vegas magic shows range from grand spectacles in custom-designed theaters to intimate close-up performances that demonstrate the subtler aspects of the craft. These shows often combine multiple entertainment elements, weaving comedy, drama, and even social commentary into their performances.

The evolution of magic in Las Vegas reflects the city's ability to support long-running productions that allow performers to perfect their craft. Many magicians develop illusions specifically for their Las Vegas shows, taking advantage of permanent installations that wouldn't be possible in touring productions. These custom elements, combined with the controlled environment of purpose-built theaters, enable effects that continue to astonish even in our technology-saturated age.

Comedy in Las Vegas has evolved into distinct formats that serve different audiences. Traditional comedy clubs offer nightly shows featuring multiple performers, allowing visitors to experience a variety of comedic styles in a single evening. These venues typically present both established comedians and rising stars, creating an energy that's different from standard comedy club experiences in other cities.

Concert Venues
AND MUSICAL
Performances

Las Vegas has developed a remarkable variety of concert venues, each designed to create optimal experiences for different types of musical performances. The city's largest arenas rival any major concert venue in the world, featuring advanced sound systems and viewing angles carefully calculated to provide excellent experiences from every seat. These venues host everything from major touring acts to special one-night-only performances by resident artists.

The mid-sized theaters found in many resorts offer more intimate musical experiences while maintaining production values that match larger venues. These spaces often feature innovative design elements that create superior acoustics while keeping audiences close to the performers. Many of these theaters can be reconfigured for different types of shows, allowing them to host both concerts and theatrical productions.

Smaller venues, including lounges and jazz clubs, provide platforms for up-and-coming artists and more intimate performances by established musicians.

These spaces often feature excellent sound systems and sophisticated lighting despite their size, creating professional performance environments that enhance the connection between artists and audiences.

The variety of venue sizes in Las Vegas allows visitors to experience music in whatever setting they prefer, from massive arena shows to intimate acoustic performances. This range of options has helped establish Las Vegas as a premier music destination, attracting both major touring acts and artists looking to develop specialized shows for specific venues.

One unique aspect of Las Vegas concert venues is their integration with resort amenities. Many feature exclusive VIP areas, dedicated entrance lounges, and special service options that enhance the concert experience. These venues often coordinate with resort restaurants and bars to create complete evening experiences, with pre-show dining and post-show entertainment options all within the same complex.

MICHELOB ULTRA ARENA.

SCAN QR CODE

- Open your phone's camera app and point to the QR code
- Wait for your camera to recognize the QR code
- Tap the notification or banner that appears to open the encoded link

Booking Strategies and Best Values

Understanding how to book Las Vegas entertainment effectively can save you significant money while ensuring you get the best possible experience. The key to success lies in knowing when and how to purchase tickets, as well as understanding the various pricing tiers and special offers available.

Timing plays a crucial role in securing the best ticket values. Most shows release tickets approximately three to six months in advance, with initial pricing often being more favorable than last-minute purchases. However, the system isn't always straightforward. Some shows offer early bird specials to build advance sales, while others maintain steady pricing until close to the performance date, when they might offer discounts to fill remaining seats.

The concept of dynamic pricing has become increasingly common in Las Vegas entertainment. Show prices often fluctuate based on demand, day of the week, and seasonal factors. Weekend shows typically command premium prices, while midweek performances of the same production might offer significant savings. Holiday periods and major events can drive prices higher, making it worthwhile to check different dates if your schedule is flexible.

Resort loyalty programs often provide members with exclusive pre-sale opportunities and special pricing. Even basic membership tiers frequently offer access to entertainment discounts not available to the general public. Consider joining these programs before making ticket purchases, as the savings can be substantial, especially when booking multiple shows.

When selecting seats, understanding the venue layout becomes crucial. Many Las Vegas theaters are designed to provide good views from all sections, making premium seating unnecessary for full enjoyment of the show. Mid-tier seating often provides an excellent balance of experience and value, particularly in custom-designed theaters where sight lines have been carefully considered during construction.

Looking beyond traditional ticket outlets can reveal additional savings opportunities. Many hotels offer package deals that combine show tickets with room stays at favorable rates. These packages might include perks like premium seating or meet-and-greet opportunities not available when purchasing tickets separately.

Free Entertainment Options

Las Vegas offers an impressive array of free entertainment options that rival paid shows in terms of quality and spectacle. These attractions have become destinations in themselves, drawing millions of visitors annually and providing entertainment value that enhances any Vegas visit regardless of budget.

The Bellagio Conservatory and Botanical Gardens presents seasonal displays that transform an immense indoor space into a wonderland of flowers, trees, and artistic elements. Each season brings a completely new exhibition, with teams of horticulturists and designers working overnight to create these massive displays. The attention to detail and scale of these exhibitions rivals many paid attractions, making it worth multiple visits during your stay as lighting changes throughout the day create different viewing experiences.

Street performances along Fremont Street have evolved into a sophisticated entertainment program featuring skilled artists and musicians. The performers undergo a careful selection process, ensuring high-quality entertainment throughout the day and evening. While these performers accept tips, there's no obligation to pay, and many visitors spend hours enjoying the diverse array of talents on display.

The famous resort attractions provide another category of free entertainment. The Mirage volcano, with its choreographed fire effects and custom score, creates a spectacular evening show that draws crowds to the Strip sidewalk. The Fountains of Bellagio present what might be Las Vegas's most famous free attraction, with water shows choreographed to different songs throughout the day and evening. These performances use a sophisticated system of pumps and jets to create displays that range from graceful to dramatic, synchronized perfectly with music and lighting.

Resort properties have also developed extensive public spaces that feature regular entertainment. The LINQ Promenade offers street performers and live music throughout the day, while various properties present seasonal celebrations that include free shows and exhibitions. During major holidays, these free offerings often expand to include special performances and enhanced productions of regular shows.

Inside the resorts, many lounges and public areas feature live entertainment without cover charges. While these venues hope to generate revenue through food and beverage sales, there's typically no requirement to purchase anything to enjoy the music. These performances often showcase incredibly talented local musicians who maintain regular schedules at specific properties, allowing you to plan return visits to catch favorite performers.

CHAPTER 5

Dining in Las Vegas

Las Vegas has transformed itself into one of the world's premier culinary destinations, where master chefs create extraordinary dining experiences that rival or surpass those found in traditional gastronomic capitals. The city's restaurants range from intimate chef's tables serving artistic tasting menus to casual eateries offering exceptional value. In this chapter, we'll explore the remarkable diversity of Las Vegas dining, helping you understand how to navigate the options and create memorable culinary experiences that match your tastes and budget.

Navigating the Culinary Landscape

The Las Vegas dining scene represents a unique confluence of global culinary traditions, innovative cooking techniques, and exceptional service standards. Understanding how this landscape is organized helps you make informed decisions about where and how to dine during your visit. Think of Las Vegas restaurants as existing within an ecosystem where different types of establishments serve different dining needs and occasions.

At the highest level, you'll find the destination restaurants – establishments that have become attractions in themselves. These restaurants often occupy prime real estate within resorts, featuring dramatic design elements that complement their culinary offerings. Many of these venues offer views of the Strip or the Bellagio fountains, creating multisensory experiences that extend beyond the food itself. The investment in these spaces reflects their role as showcases for the resorts' commitment to excellence.

Mid-range restaurants in Las Vegas often surpass what you might expect from similar establishments elsewhere. The competitive nature of the city's dining scene means that even casual restaurants must maintain high standards to survive.

Celebrity Chef Restaurants

Las Vegas has become a crucial destination for celebrity chefs looking to expand their culinary empires, and understanding this phenomenon helps explain the city's rapid rise as a dining destination. Unlike other cities where famous chefs might simply lend their names to restaurants, Las Vegas demands active involvement and innovation from its culinary stars. The result is a collection of restaurants that often represent the purest expressions of these chefs' visions.

The evolution of celebrity chef restaurants in Las Vegas reflects the city's transformation from a destination known for cheap buffets to one celebrated for its gastronomic excellence. This change began in the 1990s when pioneering chefs recognized the opportunity to create destination restaurants for an increasingly sophisticated audience. Today, the presence of a restaurant helmed by a renowned chef has become almost mandatory for luxury resorts.

These establishments typically fall into several categories. Flagship restaurants represent the chef's highest culinary aspirations, often featuring tasting menus that showcase their signature techniques and dishes.

These venues become stages for culinary theater, where every detail from the plate presentation to the dining room design contributes to the overall experience.

Secondary concepts from celebrity chefs often provide more accessible ways to experience their cuisine. These might include bistro-style restaurants, steakhouses, or casual eateries that maintain high standards while offering more approachable menus and prices. Many chefs use these venues to experiment with different cuisines or dining styles while maintaining the quality their names represent.

The competitive nature of the Las Vegas dining scene means that celebrity chef restaurants must constantly innovate to remain relevant. This drive for excellence benefits diners, as restaurants regularly update their menus, introduce new techniques, and enhance their service standards. Many chefs use their Las Vegas locations to debut new dishes or concepts before introducing them at their other restaurants around the world.

Understanding the rhythm of celebrity chef restaurants helps in planning your dining experiences. Many offer lunch service with more accessible pricing, while others create special menus for pre-theater dining or late-night service. Some venues also offer bar menus that let you sample their cuisine without committing to a full dining experience.

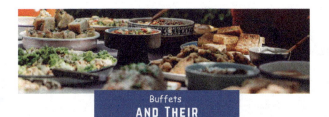

Buffets
AND THEIR
Evolution

The Las Vegas buffet has undergone a remarkable transformation from its humble origins as a way to keep gamblers fed and happy. Today's Las Vegas buffets represent culinary destinations in their own right, offering sophisticated cuisine that rivals traditional restaurants in quality while maintaining the variety and abundance that made them famous.

Modern Las Vegas buffets have elevated their offerings through several key innovations. Live cooking stations now feature chefs preparing dishes to order, ensuring freshness and customization. Premium ingredients, from king crab legs to prime rib, appear regularly on buffet lines, especially during dinner service. The presentation has evolved to emphasize smaller portions refreshed more frequently, maintaining quality while reducing waste.

The design of buffet restaurants has also transformed dramatically. Gone are the cafeteria-style rooms of the past, replaced by elegant dining spaces with sophisticated lighting and decor. Many now feature distinct dining areas that create more intimate atmospheres, while the food stations themselves are arranged to improve traffic flow and reduce waiting times.

Hidden Gems and Local Favorites

Beyond the glittering lights of the Strip lies a vibrant local dining scene filled with exceptional restaurants that often escape tourist attention. These hidden gems range from family-run establishments that have served Las Vegas residents for generations to innovative new restaurants opened by experienced chefs seeking creative freedom away from corporate resorts.

Chinatown, stretching along Spring Mountain Road, represents perhaps the richest concentration of outstanding off-Strip dining options. Despite its name, the area features cuisines from throughout Asia, with regional Chinese restaurants alongside exceptional Japanese, Korean, Vietnamese, and Thai establishments. Many of these restaurants stay open late, making them popular with service industry workers and creating a unique late-night dining culture.

Downtown Las Vegas has emerged as an incubator for innovative restaurants, particularly in the Arts District and East Fremont areas. These neighborhoods attract independent restaurateurs who can experiment with concepts that might not fit the Strip's economics. The result is a collection of unique establishments ranging from craft brewpubs with sophisticated food programs to intimate chef-driven restaurants exploring contemporary American cuisine.

Budget-Friendly Dining Options

Eating well in Las Vegas doesn't require a high-roller's budget. The city offers numerous options for enjoying quality meals at reasonable prices, particularly if you're willing to explore beyond the main tourist corridors. Understanding how to find these values helps you maintain your dining budget while still enjoying memorable meals.

Many high-end restaurants offer lunch service at significantly reduced prices, often featuring similar dishes to their dinner menus. These lunches provide an excellent opportunity to experience fine dining venues at a fraction of their evening costs. Look for special prix fixe menus that might include multiple courses for the price of a single dinner entree.

Happy hour in Las Vegas has evolved beyond discounted drinks to include sophisticated food offerings. Many restaurants, including those from celebrity chefs, offer happy hour menus featuring smaller portions of signature dishes at reduced prices. These deals often extend beyond traditional afternoon hours, with some venues offering late-night happy hours that cater to post-show dining.

Food courts in Las Vegas have been reimagined as culinary collections that often feature outposts of popular local restaurants alongside national chains. These venues offer quick, affordable meals without sacrificing quality. Many casino properties have updated their quick-service dining areas to include better ingredients and more diverse options, recognizing that not every meal needs to be a major production.

The city's diverse ethnic restaurants often provide excellent value, particularly in areas like Chinatown and the neighborhoods east of the Strip. These establishments typically focus on authenticity and quality rather than atmosphere, allowing them to maintain lower prices while serving exceptional food. Many offer lunch specials that include generous portions at particularly reasonable prices.

Fast-casual restaurants in Las Vegas often exceed expectations, with many operated by restaurant groups that also run fine-dining establishments. These venues maintain high standards for ingredients and preparation while offering counter service and casual atmospheres that keep prices reasonable. They're particularly good options for quick lunches or casual dinners when you don't want a full restaurant experience.

DUCK DONUTS

Duck Donuts
2334 Hempstead Tpke, East Meadow, NY 11554
4.3 ★★★★★   258 reviews
View larger map

SCAN QR CODE

- Open your phone's camera app and point to the QR code
- Wait for your camera to recognize the QR code
- Tap the notification or banner that appears to open the encoded link

Reservation Strategies

Securing reservations at Las Vegas's most desirable restaurants requires understanding both timing and tactics. The city's most popular restaurants often fill their reservation books weeks or even months in advance, particularly for peak dining times between 7:00 and 9:00 PM. Success in securing these coveted tables comes from knowing when and how to make your move.

Most premium restaurants in Las Vegas release their reservations 60 to 90 days in advance, though some highly sought-after venues might extend this window to 180 days for special dates. Setting calendar reminders for when booking windows open can make the difference between securing your desired reservation and having to settle for an alternative. Holiday periods, especially New Year's Eve, Valentine's Day, and major convention dates, require even earlier planning.

Understanding the rhythm of Las Vegas dining can help you secure better reservations. Thursdays through Saturdays typically see the highest demand, while Sunday through Wednesday reservations are generally easier to obtain. Early dining times (before 6:30 PM) and later slots (after 9:00 PM) often have better availability and might come with the added benefit of prix fixe menu options or other special offerings.

Special Dietary Considerations

Las Vegas restaurants have become increasingly accommodating of special dietary needs, recognizing the importance of providing options for all diners. The city's international culinary scene means that vegetarian, vegan, gluten-free, and other dietary requirements can often be met with creative and satisfying options rather than simple menu modifications.

When making reservations, always communicate your dietary requirements in advance. Many fine dining restaurants can prepare special tasting menus with advance notice, ensuring that restricted diets don't mean restricted experiences. This is particularly important for fixed-menu restaurants, which might require several days' notice to prepare appropriate alternatives.

The rise of health-conscious dining has led many restaurants to develop specific menus for common dietary requirements. Vegan and vegetarian options have evolved far beyond basic salads and pasta dishes, with many chefs creating sophisticated plant-based cuisine that appeals to all diners. Similarly, gluten-free offerings have expanded to include house-made breads and pastas that rival their traditional counterparts.

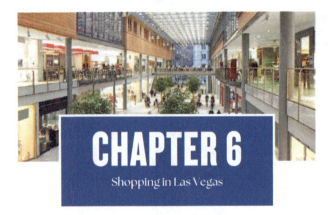

CHAPTER 6
Shopping in Las Vegas

Shopping in Las Vegas has evolved into an experience that rivals the city's entertainment and dining scenes in both scope and sophistication. From sprawling luxury malls to intimate boutiques, the city offers retail experiences designed to satisfy every taste and budget. Las Vegas has transformed shopping into an attraction in itself, creating environments where architecture, art, and entertainment combine with retail to produce unique destinations. In this chapter, we'll explore the diverse shopping landscape that has helped establish Las Vegas as one of the world's premier retail destinations.

Major Shopping Destinations

The Grand Canal Shoppes at The Venetian represents perhaps the most theatrical shopping experience in Las Vegas. This indoor shopping center recreates the romance of Venice, complete with working canals, wandering performers, and a painted sky ceiling that changes from dawn to dusk throughout the day. The architecture creates intimate shopping streets and small squares that encourage exploration, making the simple act of walking between stores an engaging experience. Live opera performances and classical musicians add to the ambiance, while the canal-side cafes provide perfect spots for people-watching and relaxation.

The Forum Shops at Caesars Palace pioneered the concept of themed retail environments in Las Vegas, setting a standard that others would follow. This shopping center combines Roman-inspired architecture with modern luxury retail, creating an atmosphere that feels both grandiose and intimate. The spiral escalator near the Strip entrance has become an attraction in itself, while the animated show at the Fall of Atlantis fountain provides regular entertainment throughout the day. The Forum Shops demonstrate how careful attention to design details can elevate the shopping experience beyond simple retail.

GRAND CANAL SHOPPES

Grand Canal Shoppes at The V...
3377 Las Vegas Blvd S Suite 2600,
Las Vegas, NV 89109

4.6 ★★★★★ 16,518 reviews

View larger map

Grand Canal Shoppes
at The Venetian Resort...

SCAN QR CODE

- Open your phone's camera app and point to the QR code
- Wait for your camera to recognize the QR code
- Tap the notification or banner that appears to open the encoded link

Luxury Brand Locations

Las Vegas has become a crucial market for luxury brands, with many maintaining multiple locations throughout the city to serve different customer bases. Understanding this landscape helps shoppers choose the most appropriate venue for their needs, whether they're seeking specific items or browsing for inspiration.

Via Bellagio represents one of the most refined luxury shopping environments in Las Vegas. The collection of boutiques lining the path to the Bellagio Conservatory creates an intimate shopping experience that feels more like a European luxury street than a traditional retail venue. The careful curation of brands and the integration with the hotel's art program creates an atmosphere of sophisticated exclusivity. The relatively small scale of Via Bellagio allows for more personalized service, with many shops offering private shopping experiences by appointment.

The Wynn and Encore Esplanades offer another take on luxury retail, creating elegant corridors where natural light and garden elements soften the shopping experience. These venues specialize in unique items and limited editions often not available at brands' other Las Vegas locations.

81

SCAN QR CODE

- Open your phone's camera app and point to the QR code
- Wait for your camera to recognize the QR code
- Tap the notification or banner that appears to open the encoded link

THE WYNN AND ENCORE ESPLANADES

SCAN QR CODE

- Open your phone's camera app and point to the QR code
- Wait for your camera to recognize the QR code
- Tap the notification or banner that appears to open the encoded link

Outlet Shopping Guidelines

Las Vegas has become a major destination for outlet shopping, offering opportunities to find significant savings on designer and name-brand merchandise. The city's two primary outlet centers have evolved into sophisticated shopping destinations that reward strategic approaches to finding the best values.

Las Vegas Premium Outlets North, located close to downtown, specializes in luxury and designer brands. The outdoor layout creates a pleasant shopping environment during cooler months, though summer visits require planning around the heat. The best values here often come from end-of-season merchandise from high-end retailers, particularly in designer accessories and clothing. Many stores receive new shipments midweek, making Wednesday and Thursday mornings ideal times to find fresh selections with full size ranges available.

Las Vegas South Premium Outlets provides a different outlet shopping experience, focusing more on mainstream brands while still offering impressive savings. The indoor setting makes it comfortable year-round, and its location near the southern end of the Strip makes it easily accessible for most visitors.

Souvenir Shopping Strategy

Souvenir shopping in Las Vegas requires a thoughtful approach to find meaningful mementos while avoiding tourist traps and overpriced novelties. The key lies in understanding where to find authentic items that truly represent your Las Vegas experience rather than generic merchandise available everywhere.

Casino gift shops often surprise visitors with their selection of unique, property-specific items. While these shops carry standard souvenirs, they also offer exclusive merchandise featuring their property's distinctive architecture or themes. Limited edition items, particularly those commemorating special events or property milestones, can become cherished collectibles that appreciate in value over time.

For those seeking authentic Las Vegas memorabilia, several vintage shops specialize in items from the city's past. These stores offer everything from old casino chips and playing cards to showgirl costumes and hotel signage. The Arts District has become particularly known for its concentration of vintage dealers who carefully authenticate their Las Vegas collectibles.

Local Markets and Boutiques

Beyond the major shopping centers and tourist areas, Las Vegas supports a thriving scene of local markets and independent boutiques. These venues offer shopping experiences that connect visitors with the city's creative energy and entrepreneurial spirit.

The Downtown Container Park represents an innovative approach to local retail, housing small businesses in repurposed shipping containers. This unique environment has become an incubator for local entrepreneurs, offering everything from handcrafted jewelry to locally designed clothing. The park's regular events and live entertainment make shopping here an engaging experience that provides insight into the local creative community.

Las Vegas's Arts District has evolved into a hub for independent boutiques, particularly along Main Street and Charleston Boulevard. These shops specialize in vintage clothing, locally designed fashion, handmade accessories, and unique home goods. The area's First Friday events transform the district into a vibrant market, with pop-up vendors joining the permanent shops to create a festival atmosphere.

Fergusons Downtown has emerged as another center for local retail, housing carefully curated shops in a renovated motel. The focus here lies on sustainability and community.

Shopping Center Amenities

Las Vegas shopping centers have elevated their amenities to extraordinary levels, transforming simple retail spaces into comprehensive entertainment and leisure destinations. These amenities not only enhance the shopping experience but also provide welcome respites during long shopping sessions, making it possible to spend entire days exploring these retail environments comfortably.

Many Las Vegas shopping centers feature concierge services that go far beyond traditional retail assistance. These concierges can arrange restaurant reservations, show tickets, and transportation, while also coordinating personal shopping services and handling package delivery to your hotel. Some luxury centers even offer virtual concierge services through their mobile apps, allowing you to request assistance or make arrangements without needing to locate the concierge desk.

The integration of dining within shopping centers has become increasingly sophisticated. Rather than traditional food courts, many centers now feature collections of restaurants ranging from casual cafes to fine dining establishments. These dining spaces are thoughtfully positioned throughout the centers, allowing shoppers to take breaks without needing to leave the shopping environment.

Many restaurants offer shopping center-specific services, such as text notifications when your table is ready, allowing you to continue shopping while waiting.

VIP lounges and relaxation areas have become common in luxury shopping centers, providing comfortable spaces for rest and refreshment. These lounges often offer complimentary beverages, Wi-Fi, and charging stations for mobile devices. Some are reserved for specific credit card holders or can be accessed through day passes, while others maintain relationships with luxury hotels to provide access to their guests.

Package handling services have evolved to meet the needs of modern shoppers. Many centers offer same-day delivery to Strip hotels, allowing you to continue shopping unburdened by bags. Some have even implemented storage lockers where purchases can be secured while you dine or enjoy entertainment, eliminating the need to carry packages throughout your visit.

Tax Considerations for International Visitors

International visitors to Las Vegas can benefit from understanding the tax implications of their purchases, as well as the procedures for reclaiming sales tax on significant purchases when returning home. The process requires some advance planning but can result in substantial savings, particularly on luxury purchases.

Nevada's sales tax system applies to most retail purchases, with the rate in Las Vegas (Clark County) currently set at 8.375%. This tax is added at the point of sale rather than included in the displayed price, which can sometimes surprise international visitors accustomed to inclusive pricing. However, certain categories of goods may be eligible for tax refunds for international visitors who are exporting their purchases.

To qualify for sales tax refunds, international visitors must understand several key requirements. Purchases typically need to exceed a minimum amount within a single day from the same retailer, and the items must be exported from the United States within a specific timeframe. The most important step is obtaining proper documentation at the time of purchase, as retroactive claims are generally not possible.

The process for claiming tax refunds involves several steps that should be planned in advance:

First, inform the retailer at the time of purchase that you will be seeking a tax refund. Many major retailers, particularly in luxury shopping centers, are familiar with the process and can provide the necessary documentation. Some stores may require you to complete forms or show your passport at the time of purchase.

Second, ensure that you receive and maintain all original receipts and tax refund forms. These documents must be kept with the purchased items in their original condition until you have completed the refund process. It's advisable to keep these documents separate from your regular receipts to avoid confusion.

Third, when departing the United States, you'll need to present your purchases, along with the documentation, to customs officials for verification. This step requires extra time at the airport, so plan your departure schedule accordingly. Some major airports, including those commonly used by Las Vegas visitors, have dedicated tax refund counters to facilitate this process.

For luxury purchases, many retailers have relationships with tax refund services that can streamline the process. These services often maintain offices in major shopping centers and can provide guidance on maximizing your tax benefits. Some luxury retailers also offer direct tax-free shopping programs for international visitors, handling the documentation and refund process themselves.

CHAPTER 7
Outdoor Activities and Day Trips

While Las Vegas dazzles visitors with its man-made wonders, the natural landscape surrounding the city holds equally impressive attractions. Within a short drive from the Strip, you'll discover dramatic red rock formations, ancient petroglyphs, crystal-clear lakes, and engineering marvels that complement the city's architectural achievements. These outdoor destinations offer not just a respite from the urban environment but also opportunities to experience the raw beauty of the Mojave Desert. Whether you're an experienced hiker or simply seeking a change of pace from casino life, the region's outdoor attractions provide memorable experiences that showcase another side of the Las Vegas experience.

Red Rock Canyon Activities

Just 20 minutes from the Las Vegas Strip, Red Rock Canyon National Conservation Area presents a startling contrast to the city's neon landscape. The area's defining feature, a set of massive sandstone cliffs and peaks, tells a geological story spanning millions of years. These formations, painted in stunning shades of red and cream, were created when ancient sand dunes solidified and were then thrust upward by tectonic forces, creating the dramatic scenery we see today.

The 13-mile scenic drive through Red Rock Canyon serves as the primary gateway to the area's attractions. This one-way road allows visitors to access numerous viewpoints, trailheads, and interpretive centers at their own pace. Each turnout offers a different perspective on the canyon's geology and ecology, with informative panels explaining the natural and cultural history of the area.

SCAN QR CODE

Valley of Fire State Park

Located about an hour northeast of Las Vegas, Valley of Fire State Park showcases some of the most vibrant and otherworldly desert landscapes in the Southwest. The park's name comes from its brilliant red sandstone formations, which appear to be on fire when reflecting the desert sun. These ancient rocks, formed from great shifting sand dunes during the age of dinosaurs, now create a wonderland of twisted and contorted shapes that fire the imagination.

The park's visitor center provides an excellent introduction to the area's geology, ecology, and human history. Interactive exhibits explain how these remarkable formations developed and how various cultures, from ancient Native Americans to pioneer settlers, interacted with this challenging landscape. The center also offers valuable information about current conditions and safety considerations for exploring the park.

Several short but rewarding hiking trails allow visitors to experience the park's highlights. The Fire Wave trail, added in recent years, leads to a remarkable formation where bands of red and white sandstone create a pattern resembling an ocean wave frozen in stone. The White Domes trail offers a more diverse experience, including a slot canyon and historic movie set remains.

Lake Mead and Hoover Dam

The creation of Hoover Dam in the 1930s transformed the desert landscape, creating Lake Mead and providing essential water and power resources for the Southwest. Today, these interconnected attractions offer visitors a combination of engineering achievement and outdoor recreation opportunities unlike anywhere else in the region.

Hoover Dam stands as one of humanity's most impressive engineering accomplishments. The dam's construction required unprecedented innovations in concrete mixing, cooling, and placement techniques. Modern tours of the facility provide insight into both its historical significance and continuing importance to the region. The powerplant tour takes visitors inside the facility to see the massive generators that provide clean hydroelectric power to millions of homes and businesses across three states.

Lake Mead, stretching behind Hoover Dam, creates a startling blue oasis in the desert landscape. The lake offers numerous recreation opportunities, from swimming and fishing to boating and water skiing. Several marinas around the lake provide boat rentals and launching facilities. The Boulder Beach area, closest to Las Vegas,

Grand Canyon Excursions

The Grand Canyon stands as one of the world's most impressive natural wonders, and its proximity to Las Vegas makes it an essential day trip destination. Understanding your options for visiting this magnificent landmark helps ensure you select the experience that best matches your interests and available time.

The West Rim, managed by the Hualapai Tribe, offers the quickest access from Las Vegas, making it ideal for single-day excursions. Here, the famous Skywalk extends 70 feet beyond the canyon rim, its glass floor allowing visitors to see 4,000 feet down to the canyon floor. Beyond the Skywalk, the West Rim provides several unique viewpoints and cultural experiences that showcase both the natural wonder and Native American heritage of the area.

The South Rim, though requiring a longer journey from Las Vegas, rewards visitors with what many consider the classic Grand Canyon experience. This area houses the majority of the canyon's most famous viewpoints, historic structures, and hiking trails. The Rim Trail offers easy walking access to numerous overlooks, while the Bright Angel Trail provides opportunities for those wishing to venture below the rim.

Desert Adventure Options

The Mojave Desert surrounding Las Vegas offers numerous opportunities for adventure beyond traditional sightseeing. These experiences allow visitors to engage more actively with the desert environment while enjoying professionally guided adventures tailored to various skill levels.

ATV and off-road tours traverse the desert's rugged terrain, accessing remote areas that showcase the raw beauty of the Mojave. These tours often visit historic mining sites, desert wildlife habitats, and dramatic viewpoints inaccessible by regular vehicles. Professional guides provide instruction and safety equipment, making these adventures accessible even to those without previous off-road experience.

Rock climbing and canyoneering adventures take advantage of the region's unique geology. Beyond Red Rock Canyon, areas like Mount Charleston offer different climbing experiences at higher elevations, where temperatures remain comfortable even during summer months. Guided canyoneering trips combine hiking, climbing, and rappelling to explore narrow slot canyons and hidden waterfalls.

Golf Courses and Sports Activities

Las Vegas has emerged as a premier golf destination, with courses designed by legendary architects taking full advantage of the dramatic desert landscape. The year-round playing season and variety of courses make it possible to enjoy golf in any season, though timing your rounds becomes crucial for comfort and optimal playing conditions.

Desert courses like Shadow Creek and Wolf Creek demonstrate how designers have incorporated natural desert features into challenging and beautiful golf experiences. These courses require different playing strategies than traditional grass courses, with desert areas and elevation changes creating unique challenges. Many courses offer twilight rates that provide significant savings while offering some of the most scenic playing times as the desert sun sets.

Beyond golf, outdoor sports enthusiasts find numerous options around Las Vegas. The Red Rock Canyon area offers world-class mountain biking trails ranging from beginner-friendly desert paths to technical single-track routes. Tennis facilities at many resorts provide both indoor and outdoor courts, with some offering professional instruction programs.

Seasonal Considerations for Outdoor Activities

Understanding seasonal patterns proves crucial for enjoying outdoor activities around Las Vegas safely and comfortably. The region's climate creates distinct opportunities and challenges throughout the year that should inform both activity selection and timing.

Summer months (June through September) bring intense heat, with temperatures regularly exceeding 100°F (38°C). During this season, early morning and evening hours become prime times for outdoor activities. Water-based activities at Lake Mead prove particularly appealing, while higher elevation destinations like Mount Charleston offer relief from valley temperatures. Golf courses typically offer significant discounts during summer afternoons, though early morning tee times remain preferred by experienced players.

Spring (March through May) and fall (October through November) provide ideal conditions for most outdoor activities. These seasons offer comfortable temperatures and clear skies, perfect for hiking, climbing, and desert exploration. Spring often brings desert wildflower blooms, creating spectacular photo opportunities, while fall provides stable weather patterns ideal for outdoor adventures.

Winter months (December through February) bring cooler temperatures to the valley floor and the possibility of snow at higher elevations. This season offers excellent conditions for desert hiking and rock climbing, though morning hours can be quite cold. Mount Charleston transforms into a winter sports destination, offering skiing and snowboarding within an hour's drive of the Strip. Desert golf remains viable throughout winter, with afternoon tee times providing the most comfortable playing conditions.

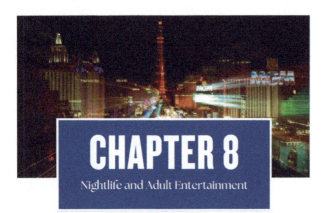

CHAPTER 8

Nightlife and Adult Entertainment

Las Vegas after dark transforms into a different world, where world-class entertainment venues create unforgettable experiences that rival any nightlife destination globally. The city's approach to nightlife focuses on creating complete entertainment experiences, combining music, technology, and service in ways that set new standards for the industry. Whether you're interested in celebrity DJ performances, sophisticated cocktail lounges, or poolside parties, Las Vegas offers venues and experiences designed to match every preference and style.

Major Nightclub Overview

Las Vegas nightclubs represent the pinnacle of nightlife entertainment, with venues investing millions in technology, design, and talent to create extraordinary experiences. These establishments have redefined what's possible in nightlife entertainment, incorporating theatrical elements, cutting-edge sound and lighting systems, and innovative design features that transform spaces throughout the evening.

The modern Las Vegas nightclub typically opens around 10:30 PM and continues until the early morning hours. Each venue develops its own personality through a combination of music programming, design elements, and clientele focus. Some clubs emphasize electronic dance music with world-famous DJs, while others might focus on hip-hop or create environments that encourage more social interaction than dancing.

Several key factors distinguish Las Vegas nightclubs from their counterparts in other cities. The scale of these venues often surprises first-time visitors, with multi-level designs that can accommodate thousands of guests while maintaining distinct environments within the same space.

Pool Parties and Day Clubs

Las Vegas has pioneered the concept of dayclub entertainment, creating venues that bring nightclub energy to poolside settings. These spaces combine elements of beach clubs, music festivals, and traditional pools to create unique daytime entertainment destinations that operate primarily during the warmer months (typically March through October).

Modern dayclubs feature sophisticated entertainment systems that rival their nighttime counterparts, with high-end sound systems designed to provide clear audio even in outdoor settings. Many venues incorporate multiple pools, private cabanas, and various seating areas that accommodate different group sizes and preferences. The combination of swimming, socializing, and entertainment creates an atmosphere unique to Las Vegas.

Programming at dayclubs varies throughout the week, with weekends typically featuring bigger entertainment names and larger crowds. Many venues offer different themes or music styles on different days, helping visitors find experiences that match their preferences. Some properties have developed hybrid spaces that transform from dayclubs to nightclubs, creating seamless transitions between daytime and evening entertainment.

Bar and Lounge Scene

Beyond the high-energy nightclubs and dayclubs, Las Vegas offers a sophisticated bar and lounge scene that caters to those seeking more relaxed or refined entertainment options. These venues range from intimate craft cocktail bars to sprawling ultra-lounges that bridge the gap between traditional bars and nightclubs.

Craft cocktail culture has found an enthusiastic home in Las Vegas, with numerous venues focusing on innovative drink preparation and presentation. These establishments often feature expert mixologists who create custom cocktails based on guest preferences, using house-made ingredients and creative techniques that elevate drinking into an entertainment experience. Many of these venues maintain smaller capacities and more subdued atmospheres, providing alternatives to the larger club scene.

Hotel lobby bars in Las Vegas have evolved beyond typical lobby lounges, often becoming destinations in themselves. These spaces frequently offer live entertainment, ranging from jazz performers to acoustic sets, while maintaining environments conducive to conversation.

Adult Show Guidelines

Las Vegas presents a variety of adult-oriented shows that range from artistic productions to more risqué entertainment. These shows have evolved significantly over the years, with many now emphasizing artistic elements, humor, and theatrical production values that appeal to diverse audiences. Understanding the different categories of shows helps you choose entertainment that matches your comfort level and interests.

Production shows in this category often incorporate elements of burlesque, acrobatics, and dance into sophisticated performances that emphasize artistry and skill. These shows typically maintain high production values with elaborate costumes, professional choreography, and theatrical staging. Many have achieved critical acclaim for their creative approaches to adult entertainment while maintaining tasteful presentations.

When selecting a show, pay attention to the venue type and show descriptions, which generally provide clear indications of content and style. Most properties offer detailed information about show content through their websites and booking platforms, helping you make informed decisions about which performances match your preferences.

Safety Considerations

Las Vegas's nightlife scene maintains high safety standards, but personal awareness remains important for ensuring an enjoyable experience. The key to a safe night out involves understanding both the environment and basic precautions that help prevent common issues.

Transportation planning proves crucial for nightlife safety. Most major venues offer valet parking, but using ride-sharing services or taxis often provides a more practical solution, especially if you plan to consume alcohol. Many properties have designated pickup and dropoff areas for ride-sharing services, often with dedicated waiting areas that provide safe, well-lit spaces.

Group dynamics play an important role in nightlife safety. Maintaining contact with your party throughout the evening helps ensure everyone's security. Many experienced visitors establish meeting points and check-in times, particularly in larger venues where groups might separate. Most clubs have staff members specifically trained to assist guests who become separated from their groups.

Drink safety requires particular attention in any nightlife setting. Always obtain drinks directly from bartenders or servers, and maintain awareness of your beverage at all times.

Dress Codes and Entry Requirements

Las Vegas nightlife venues maintain specific dress codes that help create their desired atmospheres. Understanding and following these requirements prevents entry issues and helps ensure a smooth start to your evening. While specific requirements vary by venue, certain general principles apply across most high-end establishments.

For men, collared shirts, dress shoes, and well-maintained dark jeans or slacks typically meet basic requirements. Athletic wear, including sneakers, typically doesn't meet dress codes at upscale venues, regardless of the brand or cost. Some clubs specifically prohibit certain items like shorts, sandals, or baggy clothing.

Women's dress codes generally provide more flexibility but still emphasize upscale presentation. Cocktail dresses, elegant separates, and fashionable footwear usually meet requirements. Many venues recommend bringing alternate shoes if you plan to wear high heels, as comfort often becomes a consideration during long evenings.

Most venues post their current dress codes online and maintain staff at entry points who can address specific questions about attire.

VIP Services and Bottle Service

VIP services in Las Vegas nightclubs offer enhanced experiences that can significantly improve your nightlife experience, though they require understanding specific protocols and costs. These services typically include dedicated entry, premium seating, and personalized service throughout your visit.

Bottle service represents the primary VIP offering at most venues. This service provides a dedicated table or seating area, premium spirits, mixers, and dedicated server attention throughout the evening. Understanding bottle service pricing helps in planning: minimums typically start at several hundred dollars and increase based on table location, event nights, and venue popularity.

The advantages of bottle service extend beyond the obvious beverage service. These arrangements provide guaranteed seating, often in premium locations with better views of entertainment. Your dedicated space serves as a home base throughout the evening, particularly valuable during crowded events. Service staff assist with everything from drink preparation to coordinating additional guests joining your party.

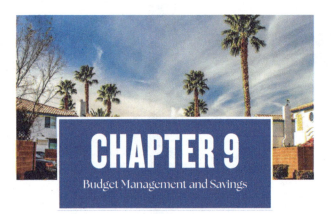

CHAPTER 9
Budget Management and Savings

M anaging your budget in Las Vegas requires understanding the city's unique pricing dynamics and knowing how to take advantage of various money-saving opportunities. While Las Vegas can be an expensive destination, it also offers remarkable values for informed travelers who know when and how to book their experiences. In this chapter, we'll explore the strategies that can help you maximize your budget while enjoying everything the city has to offer, from luxury accommodations to world-class entertainment.

Understanding Peak vs.

Off-Peak Pricing

Las Vegas operates on one of the most sophisticated dynamic pricing systems in the travel industry. This system responds to multiple factors that affect demand, creating opportunities for significant savings when you understand how it works. Think of Las Vegas pricing like a wave pattern, with regular peaks and valleys that you can learn to navigate to your advantage.

Room rates serve as the clearest example of this pricing pattern. The same hotel room might cost $300 on a Saturday night but only $89 on a Tuesday. This dramatic difference reflects not just the day of the week but also the broader context of what's happening in the city. Convention schedules, major sporting events, holidays, and even popular concert dates can create "micro-peak" periods that affect pricing across the entire city.

The weekly pricing pattern typically follows a predictable rhythm. Sunday through Thursday generally offer the lowest base rates, with prices beginning to rise on Friday and reaching their peak on Saturday. However, this basic pattern can be disrupted by events that draw large crowds midweek, such as major conventions or special events.

However, this basic pattern can be disrupted by events that draw large crowds midweek, such as major conventions or special events. Understanding these patterns helps you plan your visit during periods that match your budget preferences.

Seasonal patterns add another layer to pricing considerations. While Las Vegas enjoys year-round popularity, certain seasons tend to command premium rates. Spring (March to May) and fall (September to November) typically see higher prices due to pleasant weather and numerous events. Summer, despite its intense heat, can see price spikes during holiday weekends and special events, though midweek summer rates often provide excellent values for heat-tolerant travelers.

The convention calendar significantly influences Las Vegas pricing. Major conventions can fill tens of thousands of rooms, driving rates up across the city even at properties not directly hosting convention guests. Checking the convention calendar before booking helps you avoid unintentionally scheduling your vacation during high-priced periods. Conversely, dates immediately before or after major conventions often offer exceptional values as hotels look to maintain occupancy.

Loyalty Program Optimization

Las Vegas loyalty programs have evolved into sophisticated systems that can provide substantial value beyond traditional gambling rewards. Understanding how to maximize these programs helps you access better prices, improved service, and exclusive opportunities regardless of your gambling preferences.

The first principle of loyalty program optimization involves understanding that these programs track much more than just gambling activity. Modern programs award points or tier credits for hotel stays, dining, entertainment, and even spa services. This means you can build status and earn rewards through your normal vacation spending, even if you never play a slot machine or sit at a gaming table.

Strategic program selection makes a crucial difference in maximizing benefits. The major casino groups in Las Vegas operate different programs with varying strengths. Some excel at restaurant benefits, while others might focus on room upgrades or entertainment perks. Rather than trying to build status in every program, focus on one or two that best match your spending patterns and preferences.

Package Deal Analysis

Understanding how to evaluate Las Vegas package deals requires looking beyond the advertised savings to determine genuine value. Many packages combine flights, hotels, and various extras like show tickets or dining credits. While these bundles often promote significant savings, their true value depends on whether they include components you would actually use at times that work for your schedule.

The most effective way to evaluate a package deal is to price each component separately, considering whether you would pay full price for each element if it weren't part of the package. For instance, a package might include show tickets for performances during your intended stay, but if the showtimes conflict with other plans, the perceived value diminishes significantly. Similarly, dining credits might seem attractive, but if they're restricted to certain times or venues that don't match your preferences, they might not represent genuine savings.

Airline packages often provide some of the best values, particularly when booked during promotional periods. These deals frequently offer better rates than booking flights and hotels separately, especially for popular travel dates.

Free and Low-Cost Activities

Las Vegas offers an impressive array of free and low-cost entertainment options that rival many paid attractions. Understanding these opportunities helps you allocate your entertainment budget more effectively while still experiencing the city's unique attractions.

The Bellagio Conservatory and Botanical Gardens represents one of the city's finest free attractions, with elaborate seasonal displays that change several times throughout the year. Each installation involves thousands of flowers and sophisticated design elements that create photo-worthy scenes. The conservatory remains open 24 hours a day, though visiting during off-peak hours provides the best opportunity for unobstructed views and photos.

Walking tours of different casino properties offer entertaining and educational experiences at no cost. Each major resort creates unique atmospheres through architecture, art installations, and themed environments. Creating your own walking tour allows you to appreciate these details at your own pace while learning about the city's evolution through its distinctive properties.

Transportation Cost Management

Transportation expenses in Las Vegas can accumulate quickly without proper planning. Understanding the various options and their cost implications helps you develop an efficient strategy that balances convenience with cost-effectiveness.

The Las Vegas Monorail offers unlimited-ride passes that can provide significant savings for visitors planning multiple trips along the east side of the Strip. While the initial pass price might seem high, it quickly becomes economical when compared to individual ride-share fares, especially during peak periods when surge pricing affects car services.

Walking remains viable for many Strip locations, though the desert heat and deceptive distances between properties require careful planning. The extensive network of pedestrian bridges and indoor walkways creates climate-controlled alternatives to street-level walking, often providing more direct routes between destinations than might appear on maps.

Ride-sharing services typically offer the best combination of convenience and value for off-Strip excursions.

Dining and Entertainment Savings

Strategic timing and planning can significantly reduce dining and entertainment expenses without sacrificing quality experiences. Many high-end restaurants offer lunch service at considerably lower prices than dinner, often featuring similar menu items. These lunches provide opportunities to experience premium venues at a fraction of their evening costs.

Happy hour in Las Vegas has evolved beyond simple drink specials to include sophisticated food offerings at reduced prices. Many establishments, including those from celebrity chefs, offer happy hour menus that feature smaller portions of signature dishes at significant discounts. Some venues extend these offerings late into the evening, providing excellent values for post-show dining.

Entertainment savings often come through timing and flexibility. Many shows offer discounted tickets for less popular showtimes, particularly mid-week performances. Last-minute ticket services can provide significant savings, though this approach requires flexibility about which shows you'll see.

Common Tourist Traps to Avoid

Several common pitfalls can unnecessarily increase the cost of a Las Vegas vacation. Resort convenience stores typically charge premium prices for basic items. Planning ahead and stopping at off-Strip locations for necessities like bottled water and snacks can yield significant savings.

Time-share presentations promising free show tickets or dining credits rarely provide value commensurate with the time investment required. These presentations often extend well beyond their advertised duration and employ high-pressure sales tactics that can create uncomfortable situations.

Some transportation services advertise low initial rates but add significant fees or take unnecessarily long routes to inflate fares. Research standard rates between common destinations and use established services with transparent pricing to avoid these situations.

"VIP Service" offers from unofficial street promoters should be approached with caution. Legitimate VIP services are typically arranged through official hotel or club channels. Street promoters might promise special access or deals that don't materialize, often after collecting non-refundable fees.

B	T	Y	B	J	A	H	V	G	M	K	V	T	I	Z	R	I	H
T	K	K	E	C	A	L	A	P	S	R	A	S	E	A	C	G	O
S	V	H	U	W	C	Z	B	A	T	H	D	U	N	A	L	M	A
G	C	X	L	O	A	S	U	T	N	L	D	Y	W	U	G	I	S
I	M	W	O	U	Q	S	T	R	I	P	N	M	Q	M	R	A	V
O	C	G	U	I	M	B	S	A	Q	I	E	D	G	S	G	Z	M
B	S	A	N	S	M	Y	E	M	V	Q	R	R	C	E	Q	G	F
J	L	B	G	I	S	V	C	L	B	O	A	Y	V	N	S	O	P
C	Z	O	E	P	F	Y	V	G	L	N	S	S	D	D	A	E	B
X	Y	M	M	S	I	R	A	P	D	A	A	G	I	D	G	P	B
N	F	T	M	M	R	M	Z	K	P	L	G	C	L	J	E	S	U
E	O	X	O	S	K	V	S	H	M	D	E	I	T	E	V	J	R
H	N	W	F	T	Q	P	D	X	O	Y	T	Z	O	N	T	F	W
V	J	I	X	V	I	H	Z	Q	C	Z	Q	E	Q	N	S	O	Q
E	Z	T	O	H	Z	G	T	R	L	B	K	B	O	J	A	C	H
F	N	X	C	Q	H	N	V	N	W	I	L	K	R	C	J	B	X
T	W	T	H	E	V	E	N	E	T	I	A	N	W	Y	N	N	M

FIND THE FOLLOWING WORDS

• Bellagio	
• Caesars Palace	
• MGM Grand	
• The Venetian	
• Wynn	
• Paris Las Vegas	
• Resort	
• Fortune	
• Showgirl	
• Dealer	
• Gamble	

• Dice	
• chips	
• strip	
• hotel	
• lounge	
• Vegas	

QUICK TIPS

Tick the check box to
confirm any found word

CHAPTER 10
Practical Tips and Local Knowledge

Successfully navigating Las Vegas requires understanding more than just its attractions and entertainment options. The city operates with its own unique customs, rhythms, and environmental challenges that can significantly impact your experience. In this chapter, we'll explore the essential practical knowledge that helps you handle everyday situations confidently while staying safe and comfortable throughout your visit. Whether you're wondering about tipping customs, safety considerations, or dealing with the desert climate, these insights will help you manage your visit like a seasoned local.

Tipping Guidelines and Etiquette

Tipping in Las Vegas follows patterns that might differ from what you're accustomed to in other cities. The service industry forms the backbone of Las Vegas's economy, and understanding proper tipping practices helps ensure good service while appropriately acknowledging the hard work of service professionals. Consider tipping not just as an optional extra but as an integral part of the cost of various services in Las Vegas.

Hotel services require particular attention to tipping customs. Bellhops typically expect $2-3 per bag, with a minimum of $5 for any service call. Housekeeping deserves special consideration – a daily tip of $3-5 is appropriate for standard rooms, with higher amounts for suites or special requests. Leaving the tip daily, rather than at the end of your stay, ensures it reaches the specific staff member who cleaned your room that day.

Restaurant tipping in Las Vegas generally starts at 20% for satisfactory service, with many locals tipping more for exceptional experiences. This slightly higher standard reflects both the high level of service typically provided and the importance of service industry wages to the local economy.

Safety and Security Measures

Las Vegas maintains sophisticated security systems throughout its tourist corridors, but personal awareness remains essential for a safe visit. Understanding both the obvious and subtle aspects of Las Vegas safety helps you avoid potential issues while feeling confident exploring the city.

Hotel security starts with proper management of your room key. Modern hotels encode new keys for each guest, deactivating previous keys. Never leave your key where others might see your room number, and if you lose a key, report it immediately. Hotels will quickly provide a new key with a different electronic code, invalidating the lost one.

Walking the Strip requires attention to both traffic and personal safety. Use pedestrian bridges whenever possible – they're not just for convenience but provide safer passage across busy intersections. While the Strip remains well-patrolled, maintain awareness of your surroundings, particularly late at night or when walking through less crowded areas.

Financial security deserves special attention in Las Vegas. Use casino cages rather than standard ATMs for cash withdrawals when possible – their fees are often lower, and the transactions are more secure.

Weather Preparation

The desert environment of Las Vegas creates unique challenges that require specific preparation. Understanding how to manage the climate helps you stay comfortable while enjoying outdoor activities throughout your visit.

Hydration becomes crucial in Las Vegas's arid climate. The dry air causes perspiration to evaporate so quickly you might not realize how much fluid you're losing. Plan to drink significantly more water than usual – a good rule of thumb is one bottle of water per hour when outdoors in warm weather. Many hotels provide complimentary bottles of water to guests; take advantage of these offers and keep water with you constantly.

Sun protection requires a comprehensive approach in the desert environment. The combination of elevation, clear skies, and reflective surfaces creates intense sun exposure. Use broad-spectrum sunscreen with at least SPF 30, reapplying every two hours or more frequently when swimming or perspiring heavily. Don't forget often-missed areas like ears, neck, and the tops of feet when wearing sandals.

Temperature variations between indoor and outdoor environments can be extreme. Casinos and hotels maintain cool temperatures year-round, often around 70°F (21°C), while outdoor temperatures can exceed 100°F (38°C) in summer. This difference can be physically stressful, so carry a light jacket or sweater even in summer months. The jacket also helps with sun protection when walking between destinations.

Local Laws and Regulations

Understanding Las Vegas's local laws helps you enjoy the city's freedoms while avoiding unintentional violations. While Las Vegas maintains a reputation for relaxed rules in some areas, it operates under specific regulations designed to protect both visitors and residents. Let's explore the key legal considerations that affect visitors to ensure your stay remains both enjoyable and lawful.

The open container law in Las Vegas deserves special attention because it often surprises visitors. While you can walk along the Strip with alcoholic beverages, these must be in special plastic containers provided by licensed establishments. Glass containers and cans are prohibited on the Strip and downtown, regardless of their contents. Additionally, you must obtain these beverages from licensed venues – bringing your own alcohol to consume in public areas isn't permitted.

Photography regulations in Las Vegas can seem complex but exist for good reasons. Most public areas allow photography, but many properties have specific rules about professional equipment or commercial photography. Casinos generally prohibit photography of gaming areas, and many shows ban photography entirely.

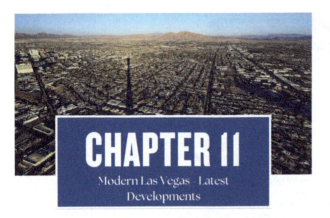

CHAPTER 11
Modern Las Vegas - Latest Developments

Las Vegas continues to reinvent itself, embracing innovation while honoring its entertainment heritage. The city's evolution reflects broader changes in how people travel, socialize, and seek entertainment, with new developments focusing on creating more diverse and sustainable experiences. This constant evolution ensures that each visit to Las Vegas offers something new to discover, while the city's fundamental appeal as an entertainment destination remains unchanged.

Recent Casino and Hotel Openings

The latest generation of Las Vegas resorts represents a fundamental shift in how the city approaches hospitality and entertainment. These new properties integrate technology, sustainability, and diverse entertainment options in ways that previous generations of resorts never imagined. The emphasis has shifted from themed environments to more sophisticated, integrated experiences that appeal to a broader range of visitors.

Resorts World Las Vegas exemplifies this new approach to resort development. As the first ground-up resort constructed on the Strip in over a decade, it introduced several innovations that are reshaping expectations for Las Vegas properties. The resort's multi-hotel concept allows guests to choose from different luxury brands within the same complex, each offering distinct experiences while sharing premium amenities. This approach provides more specialized service while maintaining the operational efficiency of a large resort.

The design of modern Las Vegas resorts increasingly emphasizes non-gaming amenities. While casinos remain important, new properties dedicate more space to entertainment venues, restaurants, and social spaces.

Technology Integration in Vegas Experience

Technology has become integral to the modern Las Vegas experience, transforming how visitors interact with the city's attractions and services. This integration extends far beyond simple convenience features, creating new possibilities for entertainment and personalization that were previously impossible.

Mobile applications now serve as digital concierges, providing personalized recommendations based on guest preferences and past behavior. These apps can track restaurant availability in real-time, suggest entertainment options based on your interests, and even guide you through complex resort properties using indoor navigation systems. The integration of artificial intelligence helps these systems learn from user interactions, making recommendations more relevant over time.

Payment technology has evolved to create seamless experiences throughout resorts. Digital wallets and cashless gaming systems allow guests to move between activities without handling physical money, while sophisticated loyalty programs automatically track spending and rewards across all resort venues. This integration makes it easier for guests to manage their budgets while accessing earned benefits more efficiently.

Transportation Innovations

Las Vegas has embraced innovative transportation solutions to address the challenges of moving millions of visitors efficiently through its busy corridors. These developments reflect a broader vision of creating a more connected and accessible city that serves both tourists and residents effectively.

The underground transportation system at the Las Vegas Convention Center represents a groundbreaking approach to moving large groups quickly and efficiently. This system, developed in partnership with innovative technology companies, demonstrates how Las Vegas continues to pioneer solutions that could influence transportation in other major cities. The success of this system has inspired plans for expanding similar transportation networks to connect other parts of the city, potentially revolutionizing how people move between major destinations.

Autonomous vehicle technology has found an ideal testing ground in Las Vegas, with several companies operating self-driving vehicles under carefully controlled conditions. These programs have helped develop safety protocols and operational procedures that could influence the future of urban transportation.

Entertainment Technology Advances

Las Vegas entertainment continues to evolve through the integration of cutting-edge technology that creates increasingly immersive and interactive experiences. These technological advances have transformed both how shows are presented and how audiences engage with entertainment.

Projection mapping technology has revolutionized how Las Vegas creates visual spectacles. This technology allows for the transformation of any surface into a dynamic display, enabling shows to create ever-changing environments without physical set changes. Properties have employed this technology not just in shows but also in public spaces, creating interactive environments that respond to visitor movements and actions.

Virtual reality and augmented reality experiences have begun appearing throughout Las Vegas, offering new forms of entertainment that blend physical and digital elements. These technologies allow for personalized experiences that can adapt to individual preferences while maintaining the social aspects that make Las Vegas entertainment unique. Some venues have introduced hybrid experiences that combine live performances with digital elements, creating shows that can be different for each viewer.

Future Development Projects

Las Vegas continues to plan ambitious projects that will shape its future development. These projects reflect both the city's optimism and its commitment to maintaining its position as a global entertainment destination.

The MSG Sphere represents a revolutionary approach to entertainment venue design, incorporating advanced display technologies and immersive audio systems to create unprecedented entertainment experiences. This project demonstrates Las Vegas's commitment to pioneering new forms of entertainment while pushing the boundaries of what's technically possible.

Sports-related development continues to expand, with new venues and associated entertainment districts planned or under construction. These projects reflect Las Vegas's evolution into a major sports destination, creating year-round attractions that appeal to both tourists and residents. The integration of sports venues with entertainment and dining options creates new districts that extend the city's appeal beyond traditional gaming and shows.

Transportation infrastructure projects continue to advance, with plans for high-speed rail connections to Southern California and expanded local transit options.

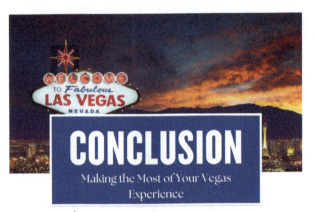

CONCLUSION
Making the Most of Your Vegas Experience

As we conclude our exploration of Las Vegas, it's worth reflecting on what makes this city such a unique and enduring destination. Las Vegas succeeds not just because of its glittering lights and endless entertainment options, but because it offers each visitor the opportunity to create their own perfect experience. Whether you seek luxury and refinement, family-friendly adventures, outdoor exploration, or non-stop entertainment, Las Vegas provides the setting and resources to make your vision reality.

Understanding Las Vegas begins with appreciating its remarkable ability to operate on multiple levels simultaneously. At any given moment, visitors might find themselves enjoying a Michelin-starred meal while others experience casual buffets, some might attend Broadway-caliber shows while others explore historic downtown, and still others might trek through red rock canyons.

Success in Las Vegas comes from thoughtful planning combined with the flexibility to embrace spontaneous opportunities. The city rewards those who do their homework – knowing when to book shows, understanding peak periods for different activities, and recognizing value opportunities can significantly enhance your experience. However, equally important is maintaining the openness to discover unexpected pleasures, whether that's a restaurant recommendation from a local, an impromptu show decision, or a spontaneous adventure beyond the Strip.

The key to maximizing your Las Vegas experience lies in finding your personal balance. This might mean mixing luxury experiences with budget-friendly options, combining planned activities with free time for exploration, or alternating high-energy entertainment with peaceful moments. Remember that Las Vegas operates 24 hours a day, allowing you to set your own pace and schedule. There's no need to try everything in one visit – many find that Las Vegas becomes more enjoyable as they return and discover new aspects of the city.

Consider, too, that Las Vegas constantly evolves while maintaining its core appeal. New attractions, shows, and restaurants regularly debut, while established favorites continuously refresh their offerings. This perpetual evolution means that even frequent visitors can discover something new with each trip. Staying informed about recent developments helps you take advantage of the latest offerings while understanding the city's timeless attractions helps you appreciate its enduring magic.

Remember that Las Vegas exists to create memorable experiences. The city's service professionals, from hotel staff to performers to restaurant servers, understand their role in making your visit special. Don't hesitate to ask for recommendations, express preferences, or seek assistance – Las Vegas thrives on helping visitors realize their perfect vacation vision.

As you plan your visit, remember that the most successful Las Vegas experiences often come from balancing ambition with reality. While the city offers endless possibilities, trying to do everything in one trip often leads to exhaustion rather than enjoyment. Instead, consider what matters most to you – whether that's entertainment, dining, relaxation, or adventure – and build your plan around those priorities while leaving room for discovery.

Finally, approach Las Vegas with an open mind and a sense of adventure. The city's reputation for excess sometimes overshadows its remarkable depth and sophistication. Beyond the famous casinos lie world-class art collections, innovative technological attractions, cultural landmarks, and natural wonders. Las Vegas rewards curiosity, offering surprising discoveries for those willing to look beyond the obvious and explore its many layers.

Your Las Vegas experience will be uniquely yours, shaped by your interests, choices, and discoveries. Use this guide as a foundation for understanding the city's possibilities, but feel free to chart your own course. Welcome to Las Vegas – your adventure awaits.

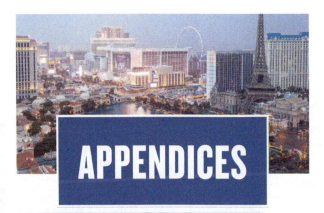

APPENDICES

Trip Planning Checklists

Three Months Before:
    Book flights
    Reserve hotel rooms
    Research show availability
    Consider travel insurance
    Check convention calendar for dates
    Join hotel loyalty programs
    Research restaurant options

One Month Before:
    Book show tickets
    Make dinner reservations
    Plan daily activities
    Book airport transportation
    Reserve day trips or tours
    Book spa appointments

Reserve golf tee times if needed
Check passport/ID expiration dates

One Week Before:
Confirm all reservations
Check weather forecast
Download relevant apps
Set up digital payment methods
Create packing list
Arrange pet/house sitter if needed
Print or save confirmation numbers
Make copies of important documents

Day Before:
Check in for flight
Charge all devices
Pack medications in carry-on
Set up transportation to airport
Pack according to weather forecast
Organize travel documents
Prepare carry-on essentials
Set up phone for travel

Contact Information for Major Services

Emergency Services:
Emergency (Police, Fire, Medical): 911
Non-Emergency Police: (702) 828-3111
Tourist Safety Division: (702) 229-3709

Hospitals and Medical Centers:
Sunrise Hospital and Medical Center
3186 S. Maryland Parkway
Las Vegas, NV 89109
(702) 731-8000

University Medical Center
1800 W. Charleston Blvd.
Las Vegas, NV 89102
(702) 383-2000

Transportation Services:
Harry Reid International Airport Information: (702) 261-5211
Regional Transportation Commission (RTC): (702) 228-7433
Las Vegas Monorail: (702) 699-8200

Major Hotel Properties:
Bellagio Resort & Casino: (888) 987-6667
Caesars Palace: (866) 227-5938
MGM Grand: (877) 880-0880
The Venetian Resort: (702) 414-1000
Wynn Las Vegas: (702) 770-7000

Show Ticket Services:
Cirque du Soleil Box Office: (702) 352-0221
MGM Resorts Entertainment: (702) 531-3826
Caesars Entertainment Shows: (702) 777-2782

Tourist Information:
Las Vegas Convention and Visitors Authority: (702) 892-0711
Downtown Las Vegas Alliance: (702) 384-2484

Emergency Numbers and Resources

In case of any emergency in Las Vegas, dial 911 for immediate response from police, fire, or medical services. For non-emergency police matters, you can reach the Las Vegas Metropolitan Police Department at (702) 828-3111. The Tourist Safety Division, specifically focused on visitor concerns, can be reached at (702) 229-3709. For poison-related emergencies, contact the Poison Control Center at (800) 222-1222.

Several major medical facilities serve the Las Vegas area. Sunrise Hospital, located at 3186 S. Maryland Parkway, provides comprehensive emergency care and can be reached at (702) 731-8000. University Medical Center, the city's premier trauma center, is located at 1800 W. Charleston Boulevard and can be contacted at (702) 383-2000. Desert Springs Hospital offers 24-hour emergency services at (702) 733-8800.

For prescription needs, several 24-hour pharmacies operate along the Strip. The CVS on Las Vegas Boulevard can be reached at (702) 262-9065, while the Walgreens location offers services at (702) 732-4795. Downtown visitors can access the CVS at (702) 382-4283.

In case of lost credit cards, keep these important numbers handy: Visa (800) 847-2911, Mastercard (800) 627-8372, American Express (800) 528-4800, and Discover (800) 347-2683.

Made in United States
Orlando, FL
11 March 2025

59355100R00075